BASIC TEXTS IN COUNSELLING AND PSYCHOTHERAPY

Series editor: Stephen Frosh

C000217507

This series introduces readers to the theory and prac[tice] a wide range of topic areas. The books appeal to any[one] therapeutic skills and are particularly relevant to wor[k] related settings. The books are unusual in being roote[d] being written at an accessible, readable and introduct[ory level. Each] text offers theoretical background and guidance for practice, with creative use of clinical examples.

Published

Jenny Altschuler
COUNSELLING AND PSYCHOTHERAPY FOR FAMILIES FACING ILLNESS AND DEATH 2nd Edition

Bill Barnes, Sheila Ernst and Keith Hyde
AN INTRODUCTION TO GROUPWORK

Stephen Briggs
WORKING WITH ADOLESCENTS AND YOUNG ADULTS 2nd Edition

Alex Coren
SHORT-TERM PSYCHOTHERAPY 2nd Edition

Jim Crawley and Jan Grant
COUPLE THERAPY

Emilia Dowling and Gill Gorell Barnes
WORKING WITH CHILDREN AND PARENTS THROUGH SEPARATION AND DIVORCE

Loretta Franklin
AN INTRODUCTION TO WORKPLACE COUNSELLING

Gill Gorell Barnes
FAMILY THERAPY IN CHANGING TIMES 2nd Edition

Fran Hedges
AN INTRODUCTION TO SYSTEMATIC THERAPY WITH INDIVIDUALS

Fran Hedges
REFLEXIVITY IN THERAPEUTIC PRACTICE

Sally Hodges
COUNSELLING ADULTS WITH LEARNING DISABILITIES

Linda Hopper
COUNSELLING AND PSYCHOTHERAPY WITH CHILDREN AND ADOLESCENTS

Sue Kegerreis
PSYCHODYNAMIC COUNSELLING WITH CHILDREN AND YOUNG PEOPLE

Ravi Rana
COUNSELLING STUDENTS

Tricia Scott
INTEGRATIVE PSYCHOTHERAPY IN HEALTHCARE

continued overleaf...

BASIC TEXTS IN COUNSELLING AND PSYCHOTHERAPY

continued..

Geraldine Shipton
WORKING WITH EATING DISORDERS

Laurence Spurling
AN INTRODUCTION TO PSYCHODYNAMIC COUNSELLING 2nd Edition

Paul Terry
COUNSELLING AND PSYCHOTHERAPY WITH OLDER PEOPLE 2nd Edition

Jan Wiener and Mannie Sher
COUNSELLING AND PSYCHOTHERAPY IN PRIMARY HEALTH CARE

Shula Wilson
DISABILITY, COUNSELLING AND PSYCHOTHERAPY

Steven Walker
CULTURALLY COMPETENT THERAPY

Jenny Walters
WORKING WITH FATHERS

Jessica Yakeley
WORKING WITH VIOLENCE

Invitation to authors
The Series Editor welcomes proposals for new books within the Basic Texts in Counselling and Psychotherapy series. These should be sent to Stephen Frosh at the School of Psychology, Birkbeck College, Malet Street, London, WC1E 7HX (e-mail s.frosh@bbk.ac.uk)

Basic Texts in Counselling and Psychotherapy
Series Standing Order ISBN 0–333–69330–2
(outside North America only)

You can receive future titles in this series as they are published by placing a standing order. Please contact your bookseller or, in the case of difficulty, write to us at the address below with your name and address, the title of the series and the ISBN quoted above. Customer Services Department, Macmillan Distribution Ltd Houndmills, Basingstoke, Hampshire RG21 6XS, England

AN INTRODUCTION TO PSYCHODYNAMIC COUNSELLING

2nd Edition

LAURENCE SPURLING

© Laurence Spurling 2004, 2009

First published 2004
Second edition published 2009 by
PALGRAVE MACMILLAN

Palgrave Macmillan in the UK is an imprint of Macmillan Publishers Limited, registered in England, company number 785998, of Houndmills, Basingstoke, Hampshire RG21 6XS.

Palgrave Macmillan in the US is a division of St Martin's Press LLC, 175 Fifth Avenue, New York, NY 10010.

Palgrave Macmillan is the global academic imprint of the above companies and has companies and representatives throughout the world.

Palgrave® and Macmillan® are registered trademarks in the United States, the United Kingdom, Europe and other countries.

ISBN-13: 978–0–230–57861–6
ISBN-10: 0–230–57861–6

This book is printed on paper suitable for recycling and made from fully managed and sustained forest sources. Logging, pulping and manufacturing processes are expected to conform to the environmental regulations of the country of origin.

A catalogue record for this book is available from the British Library.

A catalog record for this book is available from the Library of Congress.

10   9   8   7   6   5   4   3
18   17   16   15   14   13   12   11

Printed and bound in Hong Kong

CONTENTS

Acknowledgements   viii

Preface to the Second Edition   ix

Introduction   1

**1   The Basic Principles of Therapeutic Practice
     and the Concept of Containment**   5
The therapeutic in everyday life   5
The roots of the therapeutic in ritual healing   9
From mastery to dialogue   12
Therapeutic dialogue   14
Containment: the basic therapeutic principle   20
Summary   23
Further reading   25

2   The Setting   26
The setting as the instrument of
     the container function of the counsellor   26
The features of the setting   27
Spatial aspects of the setting   28
Temporal aspects of the setting   29
Contractual aspects of the setting   31
The counsellor's attitude and conduct
     as part of the setting   33
The setting functions as a set situation   36
An introduction to Mrs A:
     how the client accommodates to the setting   37
Summary   45
Further reading   45

3   **Theory I: The Developmental Point of
    View and the Oedipus Complex**   **46**

    The purpose of theory   46
    A theoretical perspective on loss and attachment   48
    The developmental point of view   50
    Making sense of symptoms and the theory of repression   52
    The ego, identification with the object and
        the structure of depression   57
    The Oedipus complex   59

4   **Theory II: The Internal World and the Depressive and
    Paranoid-Schizoid Modes of Experience**   **68**

    Internal objects and the internal world   68
    Mourning and the depressive position   74
    The depressive and paranoid-schizoid
        modes of experience   77
    The Oedipus complex and the depressive position   82
    The early stages of the Oedipus
        complex and gender identity   84
    Theory and belief   87
    Summary   89
    Further reading   90

5   **Transference and its Manifestations**   **92**

    Mrs A: the nature of her transference
        onto the counsellor   92
    Freud and the discovery of transference   95
    Types of transference   97
    Illustrations of the negative transference   98
    Illustrations of the erotic transference   102
    The social dimension of transference   107

6   **Working in the Transference**   **110**

    How to recognize transference   110
    Counter-transference   111
    Working in the transference   116
    Summary   121
    Further reading   122

7   Phases of the Counselling Work   **123**
    The beginning phase   123
    The middle phase   132
    The end phase   134
    On time-limited, long-term and
        short-term work in counselling   140
    Summary   143
    Further reading   144

8   Working with More Disturbed Clients   **145**
    A therapeutic consultation with an ill child   145
    Psychosis   148
    Narcissistic and borderline states of mind   153
    Summary   158
    Further reading   159

9   The Organizational Framework   **161**
    An organizational perspective: understanding role,
        task, boundaries, culture and authority   162
    Making use of an organizational
        understanding: two examples   163
    The organization and the individual   168
    Summary   170
    Further reading   171

References   172

Index   175

ACKNOWLEDGEMENTS

The ideas presented in this book have come in large part from my experience of teaching psychodynamic counselling at Birkbeck College, University of London, and I would like to thank my students and colleagues for all they have taught me.

Preface to
the Second Edition

Revising the book in preparation for a second edition has given me an opportunity to plug some of the inevitable gaps which have become clearer with the passage of time. One gap is the lack of a sketch map of what counsellors are likely to expect at each stage of the work, something I think is of great help for someone starting out in their work. So I have written a new chapter called 'Phases of the counselling work'. I have also made some additions to the last chapter on the organizational framework, with the aim of giving counsellors some more conceptual tools with which to try to understand and manage the institutional demands which are constantly being made on them.

There is, however, one omission, or rather distortion which I have not tried to put right. I think the theoretical perspective of the book, broadly an 'object-relations' approach, appears even more narrow than when it was first written. There are important schools of psychoanalytic thinking, for example the developments in France based on the work of Lacan or the American schools of self-psychology and relational psychoanalysis, which are not mentioned at all. Other schools of thought, in particular those based on developments in attachment theory, do not get the coverage they deserve. In this sense the book does not reflect the creative energy which I think now characterizes the psychoanalytic theoretical scene, where a pluralism of competing schools has largely replaced the former rather constricting orthodoxies which dominated psychoanalytic thinking for so long. Nevertheless I have taken the view that it is more important for beginning practitioners to get a grounding in the basics of a theoretical framework rather than be introduced too quickly to the differences and diversity within it.

Laurence Spurling

INTRODUCTION

This book is an introductory account of psychodynamic counselling. The term 'psychodynamic' refers to a type of counselling or psychotherapy based on the ideas and techniques of psychoanalysis, as distinct from other models such as cognitive-behavioural or person-centred. The word 'counselling' describes an activity derived from the ordinary word 'counsel', in the sense of giving someone thoughtful and helpful advice. However the term counselling is also used to denote a profession in its own right, and here the emphasis has shifted away from the giving of advice or practical help to the idea of counselling being a form of psychological help given to people in emotional and mental distress. It is in this sense that the word 'counselling' is used in this book.

To become a professional counsellor a person has to seek membership of an accrediting body. In the English-speaking world, for instance in Canada and Australia, it is currently the counselling profession itself which sets minimum standards for the professions. However there are moves towards statutory regulation of counsellors, as is the case in the United States, where state bodies have legal powers to regulate and licence counsellors. In the United Kingdom accreditation as a counsellor with the British Association of Counselling and Psychotherapy is currently voluntary, but a process of statutory regulation of counselling is underway. In addition to those who call themselves counsellors, many people use counselling principles and skills in their work, such as nurses, social workers and teachers. So the term counselling has to embrace both the professional counsellor who sets out explicitly to offer counselling to a client, and also those in the helping professions whose contact with their clients includes a counselling component.

My aim in writing this introductory book has been twofold. First, to try to distil psychodynamic counselling, as a body of ideas and practices, into its basic constituent elements. And second, to then describe, illustrate and explore these elements at some length. The book is intended as a primer, to give the reader a sufficient grounding in the basic ideas and assumptions of psychodynamic counselling as a foundation for further study.

In describing the most basic elements of psychodynamic counselling I have adopted a focused rather than a wide-angled perspective. That is, I have chosen to look at these elements in greater detail and in more depth than one might expect in an introductory book. I have done so in the belief that the ideas involved, and the assumptions which underpin the ideas, need more than a superficial rendering, and that the significance and implications of these ideas can best be grasped through extended discussion and illustration.

I have sketched out what I take to be the basic elements or principles of psychodynamic counselling as follows. A consideration of what makes a relationship or set of practices therapeutic leads to the identification of one key element, namely the client having an experience of containment (Chapter 1). In order to provide this, the psychodynamic counsellor will strive to establish and maintain a reliable and consistent counselling setting, which will serve as a frame for the counselling work (Chapter 2). The psychodynamic counsellor also needs a theoretical framework as a means of making sense of the client's experience and behaviour. This is provided by psychoanalytic theory, the most relevant aspects of which are given in a highly condensed form (Chapters 3 and 4). Two conceptual systems are identified as having particular power to organize the counsellor's perceptions, thoughts and feelings about the client and the work into a meaningful pattern; these are the Oedipus complex (Chapter 3) and the distinction between experience in the paranoid-schizoid and depressive modes (Chapter 4). The most distinctive and potent feature of psychodynamic work is then identified as working in the transference, and its various manifestations and implications for practice are described and illustrated (Chapters 5 and 6). A brief description of the different phases of the counselling work follows (Chapter 7), from the beginning of the work with the referral of the client to the ending and its aftermath. The diagnostic distinction between neurotic, psychotic and borderline levels of functioning is explained and illustrated and some of the implications for practice addressed (Chapter 8). Finally, attention is drawn to the importance of a psychodynamic understanding of the institutional framework in which counselling takes place (Chapter 9).

A further aim of this book is to convey how the psychodynamic counsellor thinks about his work, that is, uses his perceptions, feelings, thoughts, intuitions and reactions to the client, together with his theoretical knowledge, to guide him in the way he shapes the work with each client. To this end I have made use of a number of extended case illustrations. All counsellors and therapists are faced with the problem of how to write about their work, as the bedrock to any therapeutic relationship is the client's trust that the counsellor will respect their confidentiality. My way of addressing this problem has been to make up the case illustrations I have used. What I mean by this is that all the illustrations of clinical and organizational work are based on real cases – taken from my own experience and that of my colleagues, supervisees and students – but consist of an amalgam of different clients and different counselling situations, put together in such a way as to highlight the particular idea or principle they are designed to exemplify. I have done this because the cases presented here do not have evidential value; they are purely illustrative of the descriptions and explanations given. Hence I have been much freer in changing and inventing factual and treatment details, while still preserving the authentic 'feel' of psychodynamic work with clients.

In this book I have drawn heavily on the writings of psychoanalysts and psychoanalytic psychotherapists. This reflects the fact that the roots of psychodynamic counselling are in psychoanalysis. Writing in 1927, Freud in fact wondered whether there might one day be a band of social workers who would be trained analytically in order to be able to 'combat the neuroses of civilization' (Freud, 1926, pp. 249–50). I would claim that it is psychodynamic counsellors who are the legitimate heir of this vision, taking on the task of applying the basic insights of psychoanalysis to the wide range of clients who seek counselling help.

Psychodynamic counselling continues to be inspired and influenced by the ideas and developments within psychoanalysis and psychoanalytic psychotherapy. However there has recently been a growth of psychodynamic counselling literature in its own right, for instance in the United Kingdom with the appearance of the journal *Psychodynamic Practice* (formerly called *Psychodynamic Counselling*). Psychodynamic counsellors are also guided in their practice by the professional standards and ethics set by their professional organization (see e.g. 'Ethical Framework for Good Practice in Counselling and Psychotherapy', published by the British Association of Counselling and Psychotherapy [BACP, 2002]).

As they belong to the same family of ideas and practices, the method of working and clinical thinking of the psychoanalyst, psychoanalytic psychotherapist and psychodynamic counsellor overlap at many points (Jacobs, 1994). Indeed sometimes in this book, when the context demands it, I have used the term 'therapist' or 'analyst' rather than 'counsellor' to refer in general to the psychodynamic practitioner. What distinguishes psychodynamic counselling from both psychoanalysis and psychoanalytic psychotherapy is its greater emphasis on the application of psychoanalytic ideas to the particular contexts in which counselling clients are seen. Most psychodynamic counsellors work in public institutions and counselling agencies, and a training in psychodynamic counselling aims to equip counsellors to work in such public settings. Here counselling is time-limited, and usually at a frequency of once weekly sessions. Working in a public setting also calls for an understanding of the organizational framework and professional network within which the counselling takes place, and this, in my view, should also figure as part of a psychodynamic counselling training. Those who want to work privately, in an open-ended way and at a frequency of more than once weekly sessions generally choose to train as psychoanalytic psychotherapists or psychoanalysts.

Freud famously advised his patients not to read any psychoanalytic literature while they were in treatment with him, for fear it would serve to feed the patient's intellectual defences against the emotional impact of the analysis. I am tempted to give the same kind of advice to the reader, that is if it is to be used as a substitute for training or gaining experience as a psychodynamic counsellor then do not buy or read this book. But if this book can nudge an interested reader towards finding out more, enrich the training of a counselling student or deepen the work of a practising counsellor then I would be satisfied that it has achieved its purpose.

In order to avoid the awkward 'he or she' in these situations, I have opted, as a man, to refer to the counsellor as 'he' and the client as 'she' when the gender is unspecified and irrelevant.

1

THE BASIC PRINCIPLES OF THERAPEUTIC PRACTICE AND THE CONCEPT OF CONTAINMENT

The therapeutic in everyday life

Psychodynamic counselling is a modern and specialized form of therapy, but its basic principles can be found in incidents and encounters in everyday life. Most people know what it is like to be treated by someone in an emotionally supportive or understanding way, even if they could not say what it is about that person's attitude towards them which relieves their distress or even leaves them with a sense of well-being. But it is not so easy to pick out what it is about such ordinary relationships which make them therapeutic.

Often the best way to make sense of some aspect of human behaviour and experience is through an example or a story. So let us consider what it is that makes a relationship therapeutic by imagining the following scenario.

A little girl has woken up from sleep crying and distressed. The child's crying is heard by her mother, who is downstairs watching her favourite TV programme. Worried by the child's distress, but also a bit irritated because of the interruption, she goes upstairs to the child's bedroom and tries to comfort her. She cuddles her daughter and tells her not to worry, but the child will not settle. The mother asks the girl what is wrong, the child says she does not know, all she knows is that something woke her up and she is too frightened to get back to sleep. The mother tries to talk further to her daughter, asking her whether she had a bad dream. The girl is silent again. The mother is getting a little impatient now as she is missing more and more of her TV programme and she is not getting out of her daughter what is wrong. She cuddles her daughter again, tells her she has nothing to worry about, not to be silly, and that she needs to go back to sleep. The girl repeats that she can't sleep, and now adds that she is frightened. The mother is getting more irritated now, feeling that her daughter will never let her go. She asks what she is frightened of. The girl says she does not know, but she fears something bad is going to happen, and starts crying again. Mother says firmly, in a way that closes off further conversation, that she is talking nonsense, nothing bad is going to happen, that she is sure the daughter will get back to sleep, all she needs to do is lie down and close her eyes, and anyway she is going back to watch TV. The daughter reluctantly lies down again and the mother goes downstairs.

Now imagine a variation on this scenario. The mother is again interrupted watching her favourite TV programme, but she is able to put this from her mind as she goes upstairs. She cuddles her daughter and asks her what is wrong, and gets the same reply, she does not know. The mother is curious about what has woken her daughter and asks whether she had a bad dream. The girl is silent. The mother waits, patiently and eventually the girl says she did have a bad dream, but it is too frightening to tell her. The mother asks what was frightening about the dream, making clear she really would like to know. Hesitantly at first the little girl tells her mother the dream, which is all about a wicked witch. The mother listens carefully, joins in at the really frightening parts, expresses relief when the girl has finished. She asks about the wicked witch, what happens to her and in what way she is wicked, and the little girl tells her that the witch is wicked because she eats naughty children. The mother (who may be able to see in this witch a reference to herself when she is strict) tells the little girl that she will not let this wicked witch eat her, and anyway she is a good girl so she has nothing to fear. If necessary they can talk more about it in the morning. She asks her daughter if she is now ready to go back to sleep, and the little girl says yes. She gives her daughter another cuddle and goes back downstairs to her TV programme.

We can use these scenarios to begin thinking about what it means to be therapeutic. In the first case the mother cannot keep her own feelings of impatience and irritation out of the situation. They are communicated to her daughter, through such things as tone of voice and facial gestures. The mother's feelings make her less available to her daughter and her distress, and the daughter will consequently feel more lonely, or perhaps guilty for having disturbed her mother. The less understood and loved she feels by her mother at this point, the more likely she is to be driven to become more demanding or controlling of her mother in order to try to find the response she needs. But this will only increase the mother's impatience, and so will make her even less likely to be sensitive to her daughter's state of mind. Here we can see how a vicious cycle of misunderstanding and battle for control can develop. In the scenario I have described there is a closure, with the girl lying down and the mother going back downstairs, but we might imagine the girl does not feel very supported by her mother and might have difficulty in falling asleep, or have further bad dreams about a wicked witch.

In the second scenario, by contrast, the mother is able to put her own feelings aside, or deal with them in such a way that they do not intrude upon her availability to her daughter and her feelings. This frees her to get in touch with her love for her child, which is expressed in her curiosity and interest in what is preventing the child from going back to sleep. She is able to be patient and wait until the child is able to tell her about the bad dream. She then shares in the experience with the child in a way which both takes her dream seriously, yet in such a manner that the sting is taken out of the girl's horror and fear. In other words the child's fear is given a shape and made manageable by the mother's response. The girl's fear, by being talked about and shared, has become tolerable enough for her to go back to sleep.

These two scenarios have been constructed for the purpose of illustration. Most real life instances would probably have elements from both. They are designed to show that what is therapeutic is less to do with what is done and more to do with how it is done. In both scenarios the mother does more or less the same things, spending time with her daughter and offering physical comfort. However what is different is the quality of attitude or attention which the mother is able to bring, making the experience in the second scenario a far more satisfying and pleasurable one, and almost certainly a more successful one than in the first scenario where the mother is taken over or distracted by her feelings of irritation and impatience. Consequently this mother cannot enter wholeheartedly into the bedside conversation with her daughter. Here, then, is a basic principle. In order to be therapeutically helpful one has first to be able to deal with one's own feelings, particularly those feelings which will interfere with or spoil one's ability to listen and respond to what is being said.

This quality of attention, allowing oneself to become preoccupied with the other and be open to their feelings and experience, is in itself deeply reassuring. There is then less need for overt expressions of reassurance. The mother in the first scenario tries harder to reassure her daughter. This is because her attitude of wanting to get away as soon as possible does not convey a sense to her daughter that her fear and distress are manageable. In the second scenario there is no need for the direct expression of reassurance as the mother's whole attitude and conduct is in itself reassuring to the little girl.

The nature of reassurance is illustrated in Tolstoy's story *The Death of Ivan Ilyich*, about a worldly and successful man who falls seriously ill and dies. Over the course of the story Ivan Ilyich is led to re-examine the attitude of those around him, and his own conduct during his life. He finds, for example, the reassurance offered by his family and friends to be increasingly intolerable to him. 'What tormented Ivan Ilyich most was the pretence, the lie, which for some reason they all kept up, that he was merely ill and not dying, and that he only need stay quiet and carry out the doctor's orders, and then some great change for the better would result ... . He saw that no one felt for him, because no one was willing even to appreciate his situation' (Tolstoy, 1960, p. 143). He finds comfort only in the presence of his male servant, Gerassim, who enjoys spending time with his master, for example, on occasions spending the whole night by his bedside. Gerassim was 'the only person who recognized his position and was sorry for him' (p. 143).

Gerassim can recognize his true situation, that Ivan Ilyich is dying, and is not frightened of it. Gerassim's expression of simple concern transforms Ivan Ilyich's suffering into something less fearful and more tolerable. Gerassim's honesty leads Ivan Ilyich to question his own. 'In the night as he looked at Gerassim's sleepy, good-natured face with its prominent cheek-bones the thought had suddenly come into his head: "What if in reality my whole life had been wrong?"' (p. 137). In Gerassim's 'good-natured' face Ivan Ilyich finds a mirror in which to see himself, but not as he has appeared to himself up until now. Ivan Ilyich is led to re-examine the basis on which he had led his life – for example, his wish to please others and conform to their expectations, at the cost of suppressing any impulse in himself which might have led him towards the unconventional – and to find it false.

In Gerassim's face Ivan Ilyich also finds a mirror for his true feelings, in particular his childlike longing to be pitied.

> At certain moments, after a prolonged bout of suffering, he craved more than anything – ashamed as he would have been to own it – for someone to feel sorry for him just as if he were a sick child.

He longed to be petted, kissed and wept over, as children are petted and comforted. He knew he was an important function-ary, that he had a beard turning grey, and that therefore what he longed for was impossible; but nevertheless he longed for it. And in Gerassim's attitude towards him there was something akin to what he yearned for, and so Gerassim was a comfort to him. (pp. 143–4)

What is therapeutic, then, in Gerassim's attitude towards his master is that he is neither frightened nor disgusted by Ivan Ilyich's fear and pain concerning his impending death. In simply accepting his mas-ter's feelings Gerassim also functions as a kind of mirror, allowing Ivan Ilyich to see himself in terms of his deepest feelings and long-ings, those he would normally suppress out of shame. This allows Ivan Ilyich to begin a process of self-exploration and re-evaluation of the meaning and quality of his life which, although painful, does enable him by the end of the story to face death and die more at peace with himself.

However although we can describe the relationships between mother and daughter in our imagined scenario and between ser-vant and master in Tolstoy's story as having a therapeutic quality to them, they do not constitute a formal counselling or therapy relationship. This can only happen in a setting which is formally structured as being explicitly therapeutic, that is concerned with relieving or healing emotional or psychological distress.

The roots of the therapeutic in ritual healing

The way modern counselling and therapy is structured and carried out owes much to the practice of ritual healing, a form of medicine which has been in existence in pre-modern societies for thousands of years. An example of a ritual healer at work in an African tribal society is given in a celebrated study by the anthropologist Victor Turner. The healer's therapy draws on the cultural assumptions of the members of that society, in particular the traditional belief that pain and distress can be caused by the tooth ('ihamba') of an angry shade which has buried itself in the body and needs to be removed. Turner observed a healer called in to treat a villager suffering from a variety of complaints, from pains in his body to a general sense of grievance and unhappiness.

The healer first made a careful investigation of the patient's kin relationships, noting in particular the current tensions in the

AN INTRODUCTION TO PSYCHODYNAMIC COUNSELLING

network. Each significant figure in this network including the patient was then assigned a ritual task, for example, the collecting of ritual medicines which would be used in the ritual perform-ance where the healing will take place. Finally the healer gathered together all the relevant figures from the sick man's kin and village. A series of rites then followed, with intensive drumming and sing-ing, followed by a series of cupping horns attached to the patient's body. If one of these horns fell off during the performance, the healer stopped the proceedings and looked to see whether there was anything in the horn.

> If he finds nothing in them, he makes a statement to the congre-gation about why the *ihamba* has not 'come out' – which usually entails a fairly detailed account of the patient's life story and of the group's inter-relations – then he invokes the shade, urging it to 'come quickly', and finally invites village members to come, in order of sex and seniority, to the improvised hunters' shrine set up for the shade and confess any secret ill-feeling they may have toward the patient. The patient himself may be invited as well. (Turner, 1967, p. 388)

Then the ceremony started again until another horn fell off, the same ritual of confession of grudges was gone through again and then the drumming and singing continued. In the ritual perform-ance witnessed by Turner this went on for many hours until all the participants were exhausted. Finally when yet another horn dropped off the patient's body, the healer announced that he had found a tooth in the cup. Everyone was happy and relieved that the cause of the patient's illness had now been identified and got rid of. Turner reports that the patient himself was very affected by the whole process and started to get better after the performance. When Turner visited him again some months after the ritual per-formance the patient continued to be free from pain and was living a happier life.

Here we can see that therapy takes place within a structure, in this case a preliminary exploration of social and personal relation-ships, followed by a series of ritual tasks assigned to the key pro-tagonists, culminating in a ritual performance lasting many hours. Turner describes the ritual healer as being like a master of cere-monies, as he has the responsibility of ensuring this structure is set up and kept in place. Therapeutic actions require a therapeutic setting.

10

A key part of the therapeutic process is based on repetition, the repetition of the preliminary ritual acts, and then in the performance the repetition of the process of singing and drumming, followed by the investigation of the cupping horns to see if anything had been found in them, and the repetition of the confessing of grudges. Turner notes that much of the skill of the healer seemed to be in managing the time frame of the procedure, making clear that no result could be expected unless each part of the procedure was carried out in its proper order and with proper attention to detail.

The healing is based on the ancient principle of catharsis, the idea of purifying the emotions through dramatic expression. Both before and during the performance the healer made clear to all those involved that the tooth would not allow itself to be caught until every ill-wisher in the village or kin-group had 'made his liver white' towards the patient. The patient too had to acknowledge his own grudges against his neighbours and relatives if he was to be rid of the bite of the 'ihamba'.

The cathartic expression of feelings, especially hostile and envious ones, is given shape and meaning by being part of a symbolic language. The patient's assorted ills, which we would probably designate as a mixture of neurotic and psychosomatic complaints, are brought into a comprehensive symbolic system or narrative structure which renders his suffering meaningful and hence tolerable. The success of the whole process depended on the healer's ability to endow the components of the basic structure – the time frame, the physical setting in which the ritual performance took place, the actions and language – with a particular quality and significance. In ancient or religious healing practices this quality could be called the sacred.

The modern therapist, including the psychodynamic counsellor, draws on similar principles. The time frame of the counselling is invested with particular importance, although it has an extended rather than a concentrated form in requiring the client to attend regular sessions at the same time each week. This ritualized and repetitive quality is also present in the requirement that the counselling takes place in the same room each time (see Chapter 2). A specialized language, that of psychoanalysis has developed to enable the counsellor to make sense of the client's suffering (see Chapters 3 and 4). Catharsis continues to be recognized as an important part of the therapeutic process, as we have already seen in the examples from everyday life where the expression of powerful and distressing feelings to a receptive listener in itself brings relief and comfort.

There are also differences between the contemporary psychodynamic counsellor and ritual healing based on ancient principles. We no longer believe in possession by the ghosts of dead people, and the symbolic language we use is more individual and psychological, to do with different parts of the mind and their interrelation. Nevertheless the metaphors of possession (e.g. in the concept of projective identification, see Chapter 4) and conflict still figure in our understanding of illness. As befits our much more individualized culture modern therapy is no longer primarily a communal affair (except in family or group therapy) but largely conducted on an individual basis, although one could say that the counsellor still has to deal with the representatives of all the client's significant figures in her mind.

From mastery to dialogue

There is another, more subtle difference between the contemporary psychodynamic practitioner and the pre-modern therapist, and that is to do with the nature of authority. The central figure in the ritual procedure described by Turner is clearly that of the healer. He orchestrates, controls and makes sense of what happens. The success of the whole procedure is dependent on his charisma. The task for the patient, as well as the other people involved, is to fulfil the requirements of their prescribed role.

We can see the same principle of the therapist as master in an account given by Charcot, a famous French physician of the late nineteenth century who gained a reputation for the successful treatment of hysteria. The young Freud in fact attended several of Charcot's lectures in Paris. Charcot advocated a technique he termed 'isolation' as a necessary condition for the successful treatment of hysterical symptoms. In a lecture given in 1885 he cited the case of a 13-year-old girl suffering from anorexia, brought to him by her desperate parents. Charcot ordered them to place their daughter in a Parisian medical establishment and then leave her and return home. As instructed the parents placed their daughter in the establishment, but they refused to leave her. The girl continued to get worse. Charcot finally visited the establishment and informed the parents that he was angry with them for disobeying his instructions and that the only chance of success lay in their immediate departure back home. Furthermore he told them to tell their daughter that Dr Charcot was forcing them to leave.

That same afternoon after the parents had gone the girl started to eat and within two months, according to Charcot, was completely cured. At this point Charcot visited her again, and she told him the following:

> As long as papa and mama didn't leave me, in other terms, as long as you hadn't triumphed – because I knew that you wanted to confine me – I believed that my illness wasn't serious, and, as I had a horror of eating, I didn't eat. *When I saw that you were the master, I was afraid,* and, despite my loathing, I tried to eat, and, little by little, it became possible. (Forrester, 1980, pp. 10–11)

Charcot's cure has some of the features we have already seen in a therapeutic procedure. His presence is such that the girl is, for the first time, able to recognize herself and her true situation, namely that she is seriously ill. By separating her from her parents he creates a particular kind of therapeutic structure, which he regards as the essential component of the cure. He functions rather like the ritual healer described by Turner, orchestrating the cure through his own charismatic authority. Indeed his reliance on his own power, as revealed in what the girl says to him, is even greater for Charcot employed no ritualized procedures and had little symbolic language or theory to draw on. The whole cure relied on his mastery of the patient and her parents.

Although Freud was impressed by Charcot's work, which showed him that a purely psychological cure of a hysterical disorder was possible, his own manner with his patients was very different. When he encountered patients displaying hysterical symptoms, as he recounted in his book written with Breuer *Studies on Hysteria* (Freud, 1895), he was at a loss to account for their symptoms. Instead of claiming to know from the outset what was wrong with them he decided the only way he would understand their illness was to acknowledge his own ignorance and to rely on his patients to tell him what he needed to know. In other words his attitude was not one of knowing in advance but of *listening* to his patients in the belief that in their speech, and their conduct during the therapy, both he and his patient could find the meaning of their illness. What Freud found was that, in the very process of speaking, the patient began to bring to light the conflicts or traumas which made sense of their symptoms. The patient's speech would be likely to have cathartic elements in it, the expression of previously suppressed feelings and thoughts, which in itself would be therapeutic. But Freud increasingly found that this was not sufficient, that what mattered was the institution of a therapeutic *dialogue* between patient and therapist.

This has become the basic method of any therapy based on psycho-analytic principles.

Therapeutic dialogue

We have caught a glimpse of this principle of therapeutic dialogue in action in the example of the little girl talking to her mother about her dream. We can see it in a much more concentrated and focused way by looking at a contemporary example of therapeutic prac-tice. I have chosen a therapeutic consultation with a young child by D.W. Winnicott where the dialogue between child and therap-ist is less sophisticated than with an adult, so it is easier to see its basic principles. Winnicott, who worked as a paediatrician as well as a psychoanalyst, evolved a practice of offering children, and their parents if necessary, a therapeutic consultation, consisting of one or two sessions to try and help overcome a particular problem. In his book *Therapeutic Consultations in Child Psychiatry* (Winnicott, 1971) he described one such meeting with a five-year-old boy whom he called Robin. He was brought by his parents as he was beginning to show signs of school refusal.

Winnicott's way of making contact with children was to invite them to play a drawing game, where one party would make a squig-gle on a sheet of paper and then invite the other person to make a drawing out of it. Each person would take it in turns to make a squiggle using a separate sheet of paper. He called it the Squiggle Game. Although the content and meaning of the drawings were part of the conversation, and were the means whereby the child became involved in the therapeutic process, their primary purpose was sim-ply to engage the child in a conversation about himself. In other words it was what the child said about the drawings, and the ensu-ing conversation between child and therapist, which was important, rather than the actual drawings themselves.

At the start of the consultation Winnicott explained the proced-ure to the boy and the Squiggle Game began. Winnicott made a squiggle of which Robin could make nothing. Robin drew a kind of circle, out of which Winnicott made a spider. Winnicott made another squiggle, a kind of sausage shape, and Robin drew curly hair on top it, and then added eyebrows and eyes and something to do with legs. Robin said it was a kind of fish. Winnicott noted to himself that this was a promising start. 'Here was a primitive drawing that was personal to him and which pleased him and he had started to play in a creative way' (Winnicott, 1971, p. 30).

This for Winnicott was a sign that Robin was now engaged in a therapeutic process.

The Squiggle Game continued and a little later Robin turned one of Winnicott's squiggles, surprisingly, into a pig with a tail. Winnicott noted that this drawing showed a sense of humour, evidence of 'a sense of freedom, the opposite of rigidity of the defences that characterizes illness' (p. 32). Robin was now thoroughly into the Squiggle Game, saying 'Is it your go or mine? It is fun, isn't it?'

As the Squiggle Game continued Robin turned one of Winnicott's squiggles into a snake, taking a lot of trouble over detail. Winnicott commented 'he enjoyed the way this particular snake had a new quality which could be described as symbolical of an erection. It was reaching upwards in a very obvious way' (p. 34). Shortly afterwards Robin again turned one of Winnicott's squiggle into a snake, this time into 'a snake curled up', saying 'it is happy' and adding 'I like that snake that is curled up'. While this was going on Winnicott noted that Robin was stroking his face and he remembered something Robin's mother had told him when she had first consulted him about Robin, that when he was a baby he would stroke his mother's face until he went to sleep. Winnicott now felt he had enough material to make a simple statement to Robin about his general problem of not wanting to leave his mother to go to school.

> ... I did refer to the happy snake in terms of himself curled up on his mother's lap, feeling safe and protected from the world. I felt confident that we had now reached a statement made by him of his conflict, a statement made in terms of going out in the world and growing up versus regressive dependence. (p. 36)

After some more squiggles, and some more conversation in which Robin told Winnicott more about his life, they spread all the sheets of paper used so far over the floor and talked about them. They found they had enough animals for a farm (snakes, spider, pig and also a goose and earth had been drawn in the course of the game). Winnicott asked whether Robin would like to be a farmer when he grew up (Robin's family came from the countryside). Robin said yes, but that there would be a lot of work to do. At this point Winnicott put an idea to Robin, continuing the theme of dependence versus independence. 'You wonder whether to go out in the world and be a farmer and work or be where you can get back to mother's lap and curl up, like a snake, and touch her when you feel like it, for pleasure' (p. 36). Winnicott added that Robin accepted this idea without any apparent difficulty (p. 36).

A little later Robin turned one of Winnicott's squiggle's into something and said 'oh, its an R but the wrong way round' and dropped his pencil. Winnicott pointed out that R could stand for the first letter of his name. Robin was amused by this. Winnicott said, 'The R is the wrong way round because R is afraid to go forward into the world. He has to make sure of being able to get back quickly to mother's lap'. Robin turned Winnicott's next squiggle into a complex kind of fish, and agreed with Winnicott when he said that the fish seemed proud of himself. Robin then made another squiggle, saying it was a better R, the right way round. This squiggle had a line going through it, and Robin said about it 'and he's got his little rifle'. Winnicott did his last squiggle which Robin turned into another snake, adding 'with his little rifle', and they both laughed.

In this part of the consultation Winnicott repeated the main theme of dependence vs. independence, again using the material brought by the boy. The now mutual quality of the interaction was emphasized by the shared humour.

At the end of the session Robin went over all the drawings again. He left the consultation contented. After the consultation with Robin, Winnicott had a brief meeting with the parents, to discuss some of the practical difficulties of getting Robin to school.

This is an adumbrated account of a consultation that lasted about an hour. The session had a clear structure, with Winnicott establishing the boundaries of time (the session having a set time) and space (the boy alone with him, the parents waiting outside). Winnicott initiated and took charge of the Squiggle Game, and brought it to a conclusion. From the material the boy produced, his drawings and his conversation, Winnicott got to a formulation about the boy's difficulties, which he put to Robin as a statement about his conflict between dependence and independence. The formulation was made in language the boy had already used – the snake, his love of animals and the R the wrong way round – and could understand. The statement made sense to Robin, who left the consultation satisfied.

Although Winnicott was clearly in charge of the consultation, its conduct was utterly dependent on Robin's active participation. It was Robin who provided the raw material on which Winnicott based his observations and hypotheses. But this was not all that Robin did. He also used the consultation to engage in a therapeutic process which he clearly found helpful. He was able to get to personal material and to find ways of expressing some of his deepest wishes and conflicts.

He was also able to use the material creatively, for example, in being able to be surprised by what he drew, and to work with freedom and humour – all signs, as Winnicott observed, of his capacity to get in touch with a healthy part of himself.

Something else happened in the consultation. Robin's conflict around dependence was not simply the topic of conversation between Robin and Winnicott, it was also an important part of what actually happened during the consultation, that is, it became enacted in the session. Robin quite quickly became engaged and then deeply involved in the Squiggle Game and therapeutic process with Winnicott. In this sense he allowed himself to become dependent. But instead of this becoming a feature which held him back, as with his mother, in the consultation it allowed him to have enough trust in the relationship with Winnicott to show signs of independence and going forward (as shown by his drawings of the fish who was proud of himself and the snake with a rifle). What was therapeutic about the consultation was that Robin was able to re-enact with Winnicott in a symbolic form his basic conflict between dependence and independence. But in the safety and creative space of the session he was able to come to a more satisfactory solution than he had in real life (see Chapters 5 and 6 on transference).

The consultation involved the active participation of both parties, who interacted in such a way as to help Robin understand and experience something about himself which he had not quite realized or been able to articulate before. This mutuality is a fundamental principle of psychoanalytic work. The method is not directive or causal, in the sense that the therapist does A in the expectation that the client will then be able to do B. The direction of the consultation is not linear because it is a conversation between two people, which at times meanders, as possible areas of meaning are explored, and at other times becomes more purposeful and focused. The role of the therapist is not to be the locus of power, authority and truth. Clearly the therapist does have authority, in the sense that he is the author of the therapeutic process, and uses his skill to articulate what may be read between the lines of what the client has said but has not yet been put into words. But his role is not to impose his truth on the client. It is rather, as Tolstoy's character Ivan Ilyich puts it, to recognize the client's situation, that is, to function like a mirror which enables the client to see herself.

Although there was physical activity in the session, in that Robin and Winnicott drew together, this was simply for Winnicott a way to help him talk to a young child. The therapy took place in the psychic realm and was conducted primarily through the medium of speech. What Winnicott did was to bring together the various strands of what Robin talked about into a coherent theme concerning Robin's relationship both with his family and with himself. Even though the consultation was with a child, who was not able to take full responsibility for his own actions and was reliant on his parents – and who therefore had to be involved in setting up the consultation and in its outcome – Winnicott did not tell Robin what to do, for example, that he must go to school. He saw his task as showing Robin the nature of his conflict and giving him the chance, with Winnicott's help, to find his own solution.

We can identify three different elements of Winnicott's therapeutic technique in this consultation. First, his whole approach and manner was designed to *engage* with the child, to establish a rapport and initiate a process of mutual interaction. He did this through his tactful behaviour and the quality of his curiosity, understanding and empathy. Nothing can happen in the therapeutic encounter without this engagement on the part of the client and much of the therapist's activity will be concentrated on establishing and preserving the client's engagement.

As well as engaging the child in a therapeutic dialogue, Winnicott also *made an interpretation* to Robin about his conflict between dependence and independence. An interpretation links together ideas or themes into a meaningful whole. A particular interpretation is a formulation or hypothesis about the meaning of some aspect of the client's behaviour or experience. It is the outcome of the ongoing dialogue with the client, using the client's actual material, and drawing on theory where appropriate (in this case Winnicott applied a simple developmental framework, see Chapter 3).

Although Winnicott's actual interpretation to Robin could be seen as the climax of the session, it was really only the most formulated expression of what Winnicott had been getting at throughout the consultation. In other words, Winnicott's whole approach – his observations, questions and comments – was to try to find meaning and sense in Robin's drawings and words. We might describe Winnicott's conduct of the whole therapy as interpretive, that is as assuming that meaning could be found in the material of the session, and directing his interventions so as to allow this meaning to emerge or be constructed.

Finally, rather like with ritual healing, there was a degree of repetition in the consultation. Winnicott's main interpretation was repeated several times in different ways, and the material of the drawings was gone over a number of times. In psychoanalytic language this process of going over the same material is called *working through*. Understanding or insight rarely comes all at once. It needs time to be assimilated, time for its significance to be recognized, and its challenge to one's pride or psychic equilibrium digested.

It may seem surprising that so much can be accomplished by 'just talking'. Freud in fact addressed this frequently voiced criticism of the 'talking therapies' in his *Introductory Lectures on Psychoanalysis*, delivered in 1915 to the public. Unlike a medical demonstration, where the patient's illness can be seen and the medical intervention demonstrated, in a psychoanalytic treatment, Freud said 'nothing takes place ... but an interchange of words between the patient and the analyst' (Freud, 1915, p. 17). He went on: 'the uninstructed relatives of our patients, who are only impressed by visible and tangible things ... never fail to express their doubts whether "anything can be done about the illness by mere talking" '. But, to Freud this is to underestimate the power of words:

> Words were originally magic and to this day words have retained much of their ancient magical power. By words one person can make another blissfully happy or drive him to despair, by words the teacher conveys his knowledge to his pupils, by words the orator carries his audience with him and determines their judgements and decisions. Words provoke affects and are in general the means of mutual influence among men. (p. 17)

Freud is here pointing to the fact that a large part of the way we relate to each other, and to ourselves, is through speech. Words are not only descriptions of things or events, they are also actions in their own right. Much of the stuff of everyday intercourse between people can only be done with words. Doing such things as making a promise, giving an excuse, having an argument or telling a joke are all activities that can only be carried out through speech. This is part of the magical quality of words, that they create a whole form of life.

Words can also be felt to be very personal, a part of knowing who we are. This is most evident in our name. In many pre-modern societies it was taken for granted that knowing someone's name was equivalent to gaining power over them. In therapy and counselling the interpretations made by the therapist, and indeed his whole way of conversing with the patient, have this personal quality of helping the patient discover who he is.

So in order to 'provoke affects' and become a means of influencing the patient, the words of the therapist need to have both this performative and this personal quality for the patient. The patient will need to feel that the therapist is interested in and really capable of knowing him. Winnicott called this attitude on the part of the therapist one of 'pre-occupation' with the patient, on the analogy of the pregnant mother's pre-occupation with her developing but unborn child.

Another way of trying to capture the transforming quality of the therapist's speech and attitude is through the concept of 'containment', first used by the psychoanalyst Wilfred Bion and now common currency in psychoanalytic discourse. It is best described through another example.

Containment: the basic therapeutic principle

In a paper called 'Keeping Things in Mind' Ronald Britton, a psychoanalyst, describes a woman in psychoanalytic treatment who lived a very restricted physical and emotional life. Her sense of her own integrity was so fragile that any change to her routine was experienced as potentially catastrophic. Her psychic world was dominated by self-punishing and persecutory thoughts about how evil she was because she had 'bad thoughts'. She felt compelled to try to empty her mind of these bad thoughts. This she did, for example, by repeatedly flushing the toilet, imagining in so doing she was getting rid of her thoughts. Sometimes she did this so often she broke the mechanism. As a result of this process she often felt her mind was empty, and she felt unreal. The world outside took on a menacing quality, and she restricted her life to a small geographical area around her house. When she came to her therapy sessions, this involved a series of rituals, of going in and out of her flat several times before she was able to leave her flat and go to her analyst's house where the therapy sessions took place. This was to ensure that she did not leave with the 'wrong' thoughts in her mind. Britton comments on his patient as follows:

> What she sought from me were basically two things. One was to find sanctuary, and the other was to find meaning. She found sanctuary in the moment she was under my roof. Once she was in the waiting room, and she always came a little early, she felt free of what she called 'the noise in my head'. Once she was in the session, she would seek meaning, reiterating, 'what does it mean? What does it mean?' (Britton, 1992, p. 103)

Britton describes 'sanctuary' as the idea of being in a safe place, being inside something good. 'Meaning', he says 'was felt by my patient to be something which would provide a desperately needed internal coherence to her thoughts, whose disconnectedness persecuted her'. Britton goes on to use the idea that a focus of perceptual experience, such as the nipple in the mouth, may provide cohesion for the baby, and speculates that this might describe the forerunner of what his patient was constantly seeking in looking to him for a 'central explanatory idea'. Together the finding of sanctuary and meaning constitutes an experience of containment.

'Containment' is a technical term in psychoanalytic language used to describe an ordinary mental process whereby a disturbing experience can be made less disturbing by putting a boundary round it. It is something that one person can do to their own state of mind. It is what the mother did in the scenario with her daughter, when she dealt with her irritation in such a way that it did not intrude upon her ability to respond to her daughter's distress. Her irritation was contained by her in such a way that the feeling lost its power to take over her mind.

Containment can also describe a certain kind of interchange between people. In this interchange disturbing states of mind in one person are conveyed to another person. During this process, as these states of mind come to reside in the mind of the second person, they lose their frightening and unmanageable quality and become transformed into something tolerable and meaningful. These changed states of mind, having been detoxified of their disturbing elements, are then conveyed back again to the first person but in a form that the person can manage. In the therapy or counselling setting containment means the client has a powerful therapeutic experience of her frightening and intolerable feelings or thoughts being held and transformed by the counsellor and then returned in a digestible form.

Over the course of this containing interchange it is not just the quality of experience which is modified for the client. It is also her belief in the possibility of her experiences being contained. In other words what is taken in by the client is not just a transformed state of mind, but also the idea or experience of a mind which can transform disturbing states of mind into manageable ones. Once she sees that another mind can contain her, it is possible for the client to see that her own mind can become a container as well.

We can see this containing interchange in the scenario at the beginning of the chapter. The little girl's disturbing feelings and thoughts woke her up as she could not contain them. She conveyed this state of mind to her mother by her crying. The mother, if all goes well as in the second scenario, takes in the little girl's state of mind. That is, she absorbs the little girl's frightening and disturbing experience and brings it into contact with some of her own good experiences, such as past experiences of having mastered fear, her love of her daughter, her memory of her mother comforting her when she had bad dreams and so on. In the course of this process, which happens outside of the mother's awareness, the little girl's disturbing experience is changed into something the mother can manage. Consequently the mother is able to be responsive and comfort her daughter. The daughter is reassured that her fears are not so frightening, that they have produced not a frightening or angry mother (as in the first scenario) but a loving one.

The term 'containment' is actually a rather misleading word, as it brings with it connotations of imprisonment, which is how it is sometimes used in everyday language. When we do think of something containing something else the tendency is to think of the container as rigid or inert, like a jug holding water. But Bion, who first described containment as a key aspect of what happens in psychoanalysis (Symington and Symington, 1996), imagined the analyst as an active and responsive container, moulding himself according to the nature of the patient's experience, like a breast holding milk. Furthermore, the container, by the very process of containing would change the nature of what is inside it. Perhaps this is easier to imagine when containment does not happen. In the first scenario, where the mother becomes irritable with her daughter, we might imagine that the little girl's fear and distress resonates with the mother's own experiences which she finds difficult to tolerate. Such a mother might fear becoming overwhelmed or taken over by her daughter's fear and distress if she were really to take it inside her. So she does not allow her daughter's state of mind to gain access into her own. The mother will then give back the daughter's experience in a similar form to which it was received, that is, with its frightening and disturbing qualities still present. Uncontained the daughter will not find sanctuary and meaning in the presence of her mother but rather confirmation that her experience is too frightening or disturbing to be tolerated.

Containment describes something which happens spontaneously, without conscious or deliberate reflection. Bion in fact employed the term 'reverie' to capture the untutored quality of the containing mind. It does not require sophistication, as in the example of Ivan

Ilyich's servant Gerassim, whose very simplicity and directness contained his master's fear of the pain and meaningless of death and transformed it into something tolerable. Containment means a form of psychological holding (this was the psychoanalyst Donald Winnicott's term to describe the emotional complement to the way a parent physically holds an infant or child).

The capacity of the therapist to contain a client can be seen to have both a psychic and a verbal dimension. To become a containing figure involves psychic work by the therapist: taking in the client's material in the sense of allowing himself to be affected by it; then discriminating between its various elements, detoxifying the most disturbing aspects and gathering the disparate parts together. Thus transformed by this mental activity on the part of the therapist, the client's material can then be given back to the client in the form of an interpretation, observation or whatever form of verbal intervention is appropriate. The containing quality of the therapist's speech will be conveyed partly through the accompanying nonverbal behaviour, such as facial expression and tone of voice, and partly through the sensitivity and appropriateness of the words themselves.

All the things we have identified in this chapter as making a relationship a therapeutic one can be seen as part of the process of containment. Allowing oneself to be open and receptive to the other's disturbing and distressing state of mind, being able to help the other recognize their true situation, encouraging the direct expression of feelings and thoughts, allowing the other to become more childlike and dependent, being interested in and curious about the other, allowing the interchange between oneself and the other to proceed at its own pace – all these convey to the client that they can find both sanctuary and meaning in the interchange with the counsellor. So we can now offer a first definition of psychodynamic counselling: the counsellor relates to the client in such a way as to give her an experience of containment.

Summary

Psychodynamic counselling is founded upon ways of relating in ordinary life which bring comfort and relieve mental pain. The qualities of mind which promote this include being sensitive to another's distress, having a concern for their welfare and a curiosity in understanding them. Therapeutic practices rely on the same qualities of attention and empathy on the part of the therapist or counsellor, but are now organized into a procedure which has the explicit task of relieving the pain or distress of the client. Traditional therapeutic procedures involve the cathartic power of language, the repetitive power of ritual and the authority invested in the healer. These figure also in those therapies derived from psychoanalysis. But in the psychodynamic therapies there has been a shift in therapeutic stance away from the idea of power residing solely in the therapist and doing things to the client, towards the idea of the therapist listening to and being guided by what the client says. The task of the psycho-dynamic therapist or counsellor becomes one of understanding the client, of gathering the client's material together in such a way as to convey an appreciation of her life situation and the meaning of her pain.

In this chapter several basic features of psychodynamic counselling are identified. The counsellor's attitude and conduct aims to *engage* the client in the process. In the therapeutic dialogue between counsellor and client, the counsellor's speech is *interpretive*, that is, it is oriented towards making sense of what the client brings. This might involve gathering disparate parts of the client's conversation together, linking together different parts of her life or personality or uncovering a guiding theme or pattern to her problems. Conveying this understanding to the client involves *working through* on the client's part, that is, overcoming her resistance to change and accommodating the insight or different perspective offered by the counsellor into her habitual way of seeing things. It is this need for working through by the client that accounts for the repetitive quality of therapy, the idea that change rarely happens all at once and is likely to involve going over the same ground again and again.

In order to be able to use the understanding offered by the counsellor and feel safe enough to change, the client needs to feel *contained* by the counsellor. Containment describes a form of mental activity on the part of the counsellor in response to what the client brings. The counsellor takes in or digests what is said or conveyed to him by the client, in particular feelings and thoughts that are too disturbing for the client to bear. In this process of incorporating the client's material, the counsellor is able to metabolize it, that is, detoxify it of its disturbing or unbearable elements and thereby transform it into something which is both meaningful and tolerable, and to convey this to the client in an appropriate form of words. It is the experience of being contained by the counsellor which gives the client the most profound experience of having been heard, thought about and understood.

Further reading

Ellenberger, H (1970) *The Discovery of the Unconscious,* New York: Basic Books.

Lanman, M (1998) 'The human container: containment as an active process', *Psychodynamic Counselling,* vol. 4, no. 4, pp. 463–72.

Pietroni, M (1999) 'Containment in theory and practice', *Psychodynamic Counselling,* vol. 5, no. 4, pp. 407–27.

Salzberger-Wittenberg, I (1970) 'Gaining insight' and 'Therapeutic interaction', Chapters 1 and 2 of Part III of *Psychoanalytic Insight and Relationships: a Kleinian View,* London: Routledge.

2

THE SETTING

The setting as the instrument of the container function of the counsellor

We have seen in Chapter 1 that whatever pushes clients to seek therapeutic help – whether it be a distressing situation, a crisis in a relationship or a painful or disturbing state of mind – what clients seek is containment, that is both sanctuary and meaning. This is conveyed partly by what the counsellor does, that is, by the quality of the relationship he establishes with the client. It is also conveyed by the context in which this relationship takes place, that is, the setting for the therapeutic work, the physical and psychic boundaries which define that relationship.

To speak of the setting in this way is not just to see it as the site where the counselling happens to take place, but as an essential part of the therapeutic process itself. If we think of the game of football, the equivalent to the setting in counselling would not only be the pitch on which the game is played; it would also be the rules of the game, together with the general principles of strategy and the tactics which make up the game, in other words how the game is organized. The setting in this sense consists of those defining features of football which make any particular game possible.

In psychodynamic counselling the setting serves to create for the client a place where containment can be found, where the client feels safe enough to get in touch with feelings and thoughts which would normally remain hidden and to find meaning in what has up to now appeared senseless or bewildering. For the counsellor the setting can be defined as the instrument of his container function (Quinodoz, 1992). It is as the means by which he can put himself and keep himself in the receptive and attentive frame of mind necessary for the provision of sanctuary and meaning. It is like a skin which holds inside it all the functions the counsellor performs and separates the site of counselling from the world outside.

In this chapter we will investigate the features of the counselling setting. It is a mark of psychodynamic counselling that great care is taken with the establishment and maintenance of the setting with each client, and that throughout the counselling much of the energy and attention of the counsellor will be directed towards preserving the integrity of the setting.

The features of the setting

Each counsellor, by the manner in which he works, creates and maintains a boundary around what he and the client do together. What follows is a list of the features which constitute this setting (drawing in particular on Winnicott, 1954, and Quinodoz, 1992). Many of the features go back to Freud's original conception of the psychoanalytic setting (Freud, 1911–13). His fundamental ideas on how the psychoanalyst should conduct himself with the patient have in fact remained remarkably consistent within psychoanalysis as they have proved to be of great importance in creating a context which is therapeutic.

Although the features I have listed read like rules to be followed or broken, they function more as markers or boundaries, together creating a therapeutic arena which can be distinguished from the world outside. Their effect is cumulative, giving shape and meaning to what occurs between counsellor and client. Together they form a container for the counsellor, providing him with the necessary context in which he can work as a counsellor.

I have grouped the features of the setting under four headings: the spatial, the temporal, the contractual and the aspect concerning the counsellor's conduct and attitude. I will list the features and then go on briefly to describe them.

Spatial aspects

1. The counsellor and client are alone together in the counselling room.
2. The room is quiet and unchanging over a long period.

Temporal aspects

3. The counselling sessions have a fixed length.
4. The frequency of the sessions is fixed.
5. The schedule of sessions is regular and fixed.
6. The duration of the counselling is agreed.

Contractual aspects

7. There is an agreed contract between counsellor and client regarding the purpose and aim of counselling.
8. Any financial arrangements between counsellor and client are clear and mutually agreed.
9. The counsellor treats the counselling as confidential, and would normally have no contact with third parties unless required by the nature of the client's difficulties and/or the organization in which the counsellor works.
10. Counsellor and client have no relationship with each other outside of the counselling meetings.

The counsellor's attitude and conduct

11. The counsellor's method is speech in the service of understanding and containing the client.
12. The counsellor focuses on the client and what she brings to counselling, he does not intrude with details of his own personal life and history.
13. The counsellor adopts an attitude of neutrality towards the client, keeping moral judgement out of the relationship and not claiming to know what is best for the client.
14. In the counselling situation the counsellor aims to be more reliable and thoughtful than in ordinary life.
15. The counsellor knows the difference between symbolic and real, wish and deed.

Spatial aspects of the setting

Those aspects of the setting which demarcate it as a therapeutic space are probably the most straightforward, and in most counselling institutions it would be taken for granted that a suitable room is available on a regular basis for clients. However for those working in non-counselling institutions, for example, as nurses or teachers, these features of the setting might be difficult to establish. They might have little choice about the room in which they have to work and may have to negotiate with other people in the building to ensure that the room designated for counselling has appropriate furniture, is reasonably quiet and is free from interruption.

This last feature, that counsellor and client are alone together, is important in fostering the client's trust. Other people will be present in a symbolic sense, as subjects of the client's conversation, but their actual presence would disturb the particular nature of the dialogue between client and counsellor. In Winnicott's therapeutic consultation in Chapter 1 the little boy Robin would not have been able to speak so freely if his parents had been in the room with him. So, for example, if the client arrives to the first session with a friend or relative and asks to come in with that person, the counsellor's thinking will be directed towards keeping the third person out of the counselling room. If he feels this can be established right at the beginning he will say something to the effect that counselling requires privacy and the client is best seen on her own. If he judges that the client does not feel secure enough to come in on her own he will invite the client in with her companion but use the first part of the session to explore the nature of the client's wish not to be alone with the counsellor, with the aim of helping her to ask her companion to leave. The psychodynamic counsellor will feel that the counselling cannot properly begin until this spatial boundary has been established.

Temporal aspects of the setting

The time boundaries establish the counselling setting as having a regular and fixed position in the client's life. The client will know how long each session is and on what day or days of the week it will occur, and will know that this schedule is unchanging.

The time boundaries have a practical purpose in helping both client and counsellor establish a viable schedule of meetings in relation to their other commitments. The time boundaries establish counselling as a continuous and developing process, as something which can only unfold over time. This process is about change and the rate or pattern of change cannot be predicted in advance as it is the outcome of an interchange between counsellor and client. The unpredictability of the counselling therefore needs predictability in the structure of the setting in order to be sustained.

The length of each counselling session needs to be determined by the counsellor and then stuck to. Probably most psychodynamic counsellors use the 'fifty minute hour', with some giving a full hour. Most counsellors find that sessions of less than around 45 minutes in length do not allow time for material to emerge and be worked through. There will be more pressure to tie things up before the end of the session, and less time to let the session develop at its own pace.

The fixed length of the session makes clear that the counsellor's attention span, his ability to focus on the client and become preoccupied with her, is time limited. It also expresses the fact that counselling is different from friendship or other forms of personal relationship in that it can only take place within a fixed time boundary. It can feel hard, even cruel to end a session on time, for example if the client is in distress. It can be very tempting to forgo the realities of time and not have to remind the client that the session has come to an end and she must leave. Each counsellor will use his judgement about when the situation demands some flexibility, for instance if the client is in no fit state to leave at the end of the session. But he will do this in the knowledge that the cumulative effect of not keeping to the time boundary is to build up a fantasy in the client's mind that she is too much for the counsellor, that her distress or disturbance is so great or demanding that it cannot be accommodated within the normal time frame of the session. So although it may appear to be more containing to allow a session to overrun in fact the result will usually be precisely the opposite, the client will feel the counsellor is unable to keep to the boundaries and will not feel safe with him. There is another danger in allowing sessions consistently to overrun, which is that it is likely to foster in the client the fantasy and hope that the relationship is 'more' than a counselling relationship, that the counsellor can't bear to see the client go. Although the counsellor claims this is a professional relationship, he acts as if it is not by giving the client more time. This is profoundly confusing if not disturbing for a client and will take away her trust in the counsellor, even though his action will seem to be giving her what she needs.

The frequency of sessions needs to be determined at the onset of counselling. There needs to be a balance struck between what the client wants or can manage and what the counsellor judges to be necessary in order for the counselling to be effective. Most counsellors find once weekly sessions to be a good baseline for most clients, and that is what is normally offered in the public settings in which counsellors work. Anything less than that will not normally allow the client to feel that the counselling is sufficiently part of their life to make a difference. The gap between sessions will probably be experienced as too great to do anything more than simply reporting on what has happened since the previous session. Clients need to feel a link between the sessions, so that an ongoing rhythm of work is established and can be carried over from one session to the next, rather than having to start from scratch each time.

The duration of the counselling also needs to be established at the beginning. The counselling agencies or institutions in which counselling takes place normally offer clients a definite time period or fixed number of sessions. Contracts of around 20 sessions or less are usually referred to as brief or short-term counselling, with one or two years counting as long-term work. Whatever the duration of the counselling, the fact that it is time-limited will have a powerful impact on the client, and is likely to bring up feelings to do with loss and death (the nature of time-limited work, as opposed to open-ended work where there is no fixed duration, is explored in Coren [2001], which also contains a comprehensive guide to the relevant literature; see also Chapter 7).

The time and day of each session also needs to be fixed. This establishes the counselling hour, for example every Monday from 2.00 until 2.50, as a time in the week set-aside for the purposes of counselling.

These boundaries of space and time have the qualities of ritual and repetition which we saw at work in the therapy of the ritual healer. The emphasis on regularity and continuity, coming to the same place at the same time each week, establishes the counselling setting as reliable and unchanging. It functions rather like the routine which each parent needs to establish with a baby or young child so that the world begins to take on a familiar and manageable aspect.

The space and time boundaries also help the client manage the transition from the everyday world to the counselling hour and back again. The fixed and unchanging nature of these boundaries gives the counselling setting a solidity and robustness which will help the client feel safe enough in speaking of whatever is in her mind, an attitude at odds with the normal rules of social interaction which operate outside the counselling arena.

Contractual aspects of the setting

These features of the setting concern the professional nature of the counselling relationship. They have similarities to the codes of conduct which are to be found in allied professions.

At the onset of the counselling there needs to be some form of contract between counsellor and client which spells out the aims and purpose of the counselling. Normally this will be in the form that the client has asked for help with a particular problem and the counsellor has agreed to meet the client on a regular basis. The contract may need to specify some of the conditions under which the counselling is conducted. For example, if a fixed number of sessions is offered there needs to be clarity about what happens if the client has to cancel a session – is that session lost or is the number made up at the end? The contract should also specify whether the counselling is to be paid for, and if so the terms and conditions of payment (e.g. most counsellors would expect their clients to pay for missed or cancelled sessions).

Some counsellors like to have agreements of this kind in writing, and sometimes this is a requirement of the institutional setting in which the counsellor works. Other counsellors find a less formal approach fits better with the ethos of counselling, which depends on both parties being in good faith.

Like other professionals such as doctors and lawyers, counsellors have a responsibility to behave ethically towards their clients and not abuse the trust placed in them. In particular they are bound to respect the client's confidentiality. We have seen how the space and time boundaries establish the counselling arena as removed from the ordinary rules of public and social interaction. If the client is to have the confidence to speak freely about whatever she chooses, especially if this concerns other people in her life, she needs to know that what she says to the counsellor will not normally be passed on to any third party.

However this duty of confidentiality towards the client can never be absolute (Bond, 1993). It is limited first of all by those responsibilities imposed by the law on all professionals, to inform social services if a client reveals details of child abuse or alert the police if a client discloses a serious intention to commit a murder. Then the institutional context in which counsellors work will operate its own policies regarding confidentiality. For example, the counsellor is likely to be required to keep written files on his clients, although clients will normally have the right to have access to these files. If, as part of his work with a particular client a counsellor communicates or works with other professionals, for example, as part of a multi-disciplinary team in a medical setting, he will need to pass on relevant information about the client. Sometimes if the client is at risk of self-harm or harm to others the counsellor may make it a condition of the counselling that a professional network is set up (see the example of Ms H in Chapter 7). Nevertheless, within the limitations to the principle of client confidentiality which are a consequence of the counsellor working within an organizational framework, his attitude is to avoid any contact with third parties unless absolutely necessary.

Another aspect of the professional and ethical responsibility of the counsellor towards the client is that the counselling relationship should be the only relationship between them. Any other form of involvement by the counsellor – for example, sexual or financial – would compromise the counsellor's ability to put his own needs and interests aside in the service of helping the client.

The counsellor's attitude and conduct as part of the setting

The counsellor's general approach to the work, his attitude and conduct towards the client also functions as a feature of the setting. If we compare the counsellor to a workman, we could say that the counsellor's equivalent to the workman's tool box is his capacity to listen and speak interpretively to the client. In listening to the client the counsellor sees a pattern and meaning in what she says, and how she conducts herself in the counselling, and in speaking he conveys this understanding to her. This is a complex process and the particular way the counsellor speaks to the client at any given time may have a number of purposes: to invite the client to say more, to draw to her attention a recurring pattern in what she says (e.g. that all her relationships involve unavailable men), to challenge her understanding of an event (e.g. that it is her fault that her boss does not like her), to express sympathy for her plight, to start to link together features of what she says into a tentative formulation, and so on. This is like the workman choosing a specific tool for a particular job.

Some ways of working do not fit into the counsellor's tool box and are not suitable for the task at hand. For example, the counsellor views physical contact with the client as a way of relating to the client which is powerful but inappropriate to the counselling setting. The counsellor aims not to touch or have physical contact with the client as this can stir up expectations of friendship, sexual closeness or the kind of physical care a mother gives an infant. None of these expectations or demands can be satisfied in a formal counselling setting. So, for instance, the counsellor who thinks he is reassuring a distressed client by giving her a hug at the end of a difficult session is actually promising something he can never deliver. There is closeness between counsellor and client, but this is a function of the intimate nature of the dialogue between them.

Physical contact is not only too powerful but also too immediate a way of relating to the client. Speech creates a space for reflection and thinking. In a conversation there is a need to absorb the meaning or implication of what is said and find a response. Physically holding or touching the client creates a powerfully charged bond of closeness, that is its purpose, but it thereby closes down this reflective space. The closeness with the client created by physical contact will implicitly convey the message that words are not enough, and so in effect undermine the effectiveness of the therapeutic dialogue.

The dialogue that occurs between client and counsellor is not like the kinds of conversation that happen in everyday life. The dialogue is of necessity lopsided as the purpose of the counselling is to help one party, namely the client. So the focus is on the client and her life. To this end the counsellor is careful not to intrude with his own preoccupations or details of his own life.

At first sight this feature of the setting can seem surprising. It is a commonly held assumption that people in distress find relief with someone else whom they know has been through a similar experience. It is certainly true in the counselling situation that the client needs to feel that the counsellor is someone who has some experience and knowledge of life, and so is *potentially* someone who could understand her own situation. But what becomes increasingly clear as the client reveals more of herself in the course of counselling is that her own life experience is unique, that it is inadequately captured by being put within the normal clichéd descriptive categories such as 'abused child', 'neglected infant', 'depressed mother' and such other. In other words the counsellor will never have the same experiences, and cannot presume to be able to say 'I know what you are going through'.

So telling the client parts of one's own life story in the belief that this will reassure the client or help her feel understood is to assume that the client is the same as oneself. It is false reassurance, for example, to tell a client who is afraid that she will not survive emotionally if her husband leaves her that you have been through a similar experience and that it is survivable, for the point is that the client has to discover this for herself. Part of this process means that the client must feel free to express and explore her fear or belief that such experiences are not survivable. If the counsellor finds himself wishing to bring in something of his own life it should normally be taken as a sign that there is something that the client is telling him that he does not want to hear.

This attitude of not disclosing aspects of one's own life goes hand in hand with another defining feature of psychodynamic counselling, that the counsellor strives to be neutral about the conflicts and dilemmas which the client brings. This is not because the counsellor does not care about the client, it is simply because the counsellor does not know what is best for the client. The counsellor may well be put under great pressure to take sides, for example against a client's partner who is portrayed as exploitative or unsuitable in one way or another. But doing so, for example, by urging the client to leave her partner, will be clinically useless, for in all likelihood this is what the client's friends are already telling her to do, and the client may well be berating herself for not being able to do what she knows is best for her. In this instance what needs understanding is why she does not do what she needs to do. If the counsellor can keep this as the focus, what will probably emerge is that the client is in the grip of an internal conflict, where part of her wants to leave but another part of her remains attached to the 'unsuitable' partner. In other words by taking sides, by acting out one side of the client's conflict – urging her to leave – the counsellor simply pushes the other side of the conflict out of focus. The counsellor's task is to help the client see and face her own dilemma about whether to leave or stay with her partner and come to her own resolution. Taking sides among the figures in the client's life is actually uncontaining, as it carries with it the implication that the counsellor, as well as the client is unable to tolerate the client's conflict. It is like a driving instructor impatiently taking over the steering wheel of the car because he cannot bear his pupil's slowness or clumsiness in learning to drive.

These two features of the setting, the counsellor's attitude of not disclosing parts of his life and his attitude of neutrality, seem at first sight counter-intuitive and unreassuring to the client. They can be read as though the counsellor should deliberately adopt a cold or even harsh attitude towards the client. But this is to misunderstand the purpose of these features of the setting. The counsellor shows his genuine sympathy and concern for the client by sticking with her as she struggles to find her own solutions, not by taking this opportunity away by imposing his own views or experiences onto the situation.

This is an example of the counsellor aiming to be more thoughtful and reliable than in everyday life. This is shown partly in practical ways, such as the counsellor being punctual for sessions, being in a fit state to conduct the session and so on. It is also shown in the counsellor's whole attitude towards the client, of taking seriously what is said, of not dismissing the client's views or opinions but rather striving to understand them. By being consistently there, on time for each session, and by protecting the parameters of the counselling, the counsellor demonstrates his reliability to the client.

All of these features concerning the counsellor's attitude and conduct assume he can tell the difference between the symbolic and the real. If the client is to feel free enough to explore what she normally suppresses or keeps hidden from herself, it must be understood between her and the counsellor that a wish is not a deed. This means that hating someone is not the same as actually harming them and loving them does not mean having to have a sexual relationship with them. This not only applies to the figures in the client's life but also to the person of the counsellor. The more the client can express her true feelings to the counsellor, safe in the knowledge that he will not act on them and will respect the difference between wish and deed, the more will she have confidence that her feelings can be contained.

The setting functions as a set situation

We have seen how the setting provides the structure and context for the counsellor to work. It is that which allows the counsellor to take on the role of counsellor. Some people may jib at the idea that counselling involves taking on a certain role, as though this would prevent the counsellor from being genuine or wholehearted in his work. But to take on a role simply means behaving in a way which is mindful of the task and context in hand (Hirschhorn, 1985), just as the same person can act in one way as the parent of their child and in another way as an adult among other adults.

The features of the setting provide the minimum necessary conditions for the counsellor to function as a counsellor. If some of these features cannot be established or maintained, for example, if there is no suitable room or a regular time available, then the counsellor may feel he is not in a position to offer counselling to a client. The setting also provides safety for the client, for example, that confidentiality will be respected, and that the client will not be burdened by personal disclosure from the counsellor.

The setting has another purpose. It functions as what Winnicott (1941) calls a 'set situation', a consistent framework which is offered to every client. What is then possible for the counsellor to observe is how each client accommodates to the setting, that is, how she adapts to its particular features. The client's accommodation to the setting will be highlighted whenever the fabric of the setting is breached by the counsellor. Some of these breaches may be lapses on the counsellor's part, for instance, failing to finish a session on time, and some will be unavoidable, for example, cancelling a session because of illness. There are bound to be breaches as the consistency which is established by the features of the setting can never be absolute.

So, for instance, counsellors need to take holidays from their work, and yet taking a holiday constitutes a breach in the regularity of the sessions. What these deviations from the norm bring to light is how the client reacts to them – for example, by denial, resignation or rage – which will show how the client characteristically defends herself against anxiety and impingement. The setting thus provides the counsellor with a consistent lens through which each client's way of accommodating to its features can be observed.

An introduction to Mrs A: how the client accommodates to the setting

We can understand the purpose and meaning of some of the features of the setting, and how breaches in the fabric can be thought about and used in the counselling by looking at an extended example.

(a) Making a contract with a client

Mrs A, a married woman in her forties, was referred to a counselling agency by her General Practitioner (GP). She had been put on antidepressant medication after complaining of feeling low and miserable, and in particular of finding it difficult to concentrate at work. When she met her counsellor, a man, in the initial session she spoke of relationships with some work colleagues being difficult, which is why she thought she found her work hard to cope with. Sometimes she found herself subject to bouts of uncontrolled crying at work, which seemed to come on for no reason. She also revealed that her mother had died some three years previously, and since then she had been subject to distressing thoughts about her mother's death. She had been signed off sick from her work but was now working again, although feeling fragile and unconfident.

In the course of the first meeting the counsellor offered a way of understanding her depression and difficulties at work as a grief reaction to her mother's death, and this made some sense to Mrs A. She and the counsellor agreed that this would be the purpose of the counselling, to help her deal better with her mother's death and its impact on her life. The counsellor explained that what was said in the sessions was confidential. He said he was able to offer once weekly sessions, that each session would last 50 minutes, the same as this initial one, and that in this agency the counselling could last up to a year. Weekly sessions were what Mrs A had expected, but she thought at first a year was much too long. She had been thinking of coming for a few sessions only, but in this first meeting the seriousness of her problems came home to her as she faced how fearful and restricted her life had become. She therefore agreed to the time frame of a year, although added that if things were resolved sooner she would want to end earlier. The counsellor agreed to this, and they fixed on the regular weekly time of the session.

Here we can see how a contract for the counselling work is arrived at. Out of a shared discussion in the first meeting the purpose of the counselling becomes clear, to help Mrs A deal with mourning her mother's death. This gives the work a definite goal, but one which is wide enough to cover many aspects of the client's life. It incorporates the issue which Mrs A came with, her depression, but puts it into a meaningful framework, the client's grief over her mother's death. The time parameters are set out and agreed. The counsellor felt no need to draw attention to the fact that the same room will be used each week as the client will soon realize this herself. The counsellor did not see the point of trying to tell the client what counselling is, as the client was getting an experience of the process in the initial session. He took the view that it was a waste of time to give a general or abstract account of counselling, which would mean nothing to a client before she had actually experienced a session. If the client had asked him any direct questions about counselling he would have given an answer along the lines of 'you will have a chance in the first few sessions to see what counselling is like and whether it suits you'.

(b) The fixed length of each session

Mrs A was clearly ready for therapeutic help as she quickly found the provision of a space to talk gave her the chance to speak about a range of feelings and experiences which she had not spoken about before. These did not concern her mother, at least not directly, but centred on two topics of concern: her dealings with her female boss at work and her relationship with her sister. It quickly became apparent that she tried to deal with her boss by continually placating her, but this usually only led to Mrs A feeling undervalued and mistreated. Her relationship with her sister was more complicated, to do with the fact that, having initially been very close, they had become estranged when Mrs A was a teenager. After a long period of having nothing to do with each other, the two sisters were brought together again by the mother's death, and this revived all Mrs A's old feelings of love for her, but also anger and disappointment with her. In the counselling Mrs A surprised herself by the intensity of her feelings towards her sister.

In terms of the setting Mrs A accommodated well to its features, finding the consistency and regularity of the sessions, and the counsellor's 'objectivity' as she called it, giving her the confidence to explore her feelings and thoughts. However there was one aspect of the setting which she did not like: the fact that the session ended precisely after 50 minutes, regardless of where she had got to in her narrative. The counsellor ended the session as tactfully as he could, allowing Mrs A to finish her sentence before announcing that time was up. Although Mrs A knew that the length of the sessions was fixed at 50 minutes, and understood that in fact the counsellor had another client booked in after her, she would often ask the counsellor something as she gathered her things together and prepared to leave. For example she might check the time of the next session, even though she knew the time was fixed, or question the counsellor about whether he felt counselling was actually helping her, even though she quickly realized the counsellor did not engage easily in conversation once he had announced that the session had ended.

The counsellor was aware of being irritated by Mrs A's reluctance to finish on time. He thought that his short responses to her questions after the end of the session would get the point over, but they didn't, and as she continued to try to prolong the session he wondered whether he should remind her that the sessions lasted only 50 minutes. But that would make him sound like a schoolmaster and was a harsh and clumsy way of dealing with the situation. He would do better to try to understand the meaning of Mrs A's behaviour over the time boundary. He then realized that a pattern which she had been describing in her relationships with others was being enacted in the counselling. Much of Mrs A's distress and worry in relationships with other people was to do with her feeling that, if there were any difficulties, things could never be satisfactorily resolved. This was the case with her boss, whom Mrs A dealt with by trying constantly to please her. She never felt her work was good enough and so would often work overtime to try to get her work right. The history of her relationship with her sister was one of periods of closeness followed by estrangement, as though they could never find a way of negotiating a viable distance from each other. With her husband there was an unspoken but pervasive sense that the marital relationship would not survive any serious disagreement between them. If anything threatened to become the source of conflict there might be several phone calls a day trying to smooth things over in order to prevent a misunderstanding between them. The counsellor then saw that something similar to all three relationships was being replayed in the counselling in terms of the fixed ending time of each session. Mrs A did not know how to satisfactorily end the session, she could not bear leaving with anything that felt unresolved to her, and that must be why she seemed compelled to find ways of keeping the session going.

The counsellor noticed something else about this situation, that the irritation which he felt as a result of Mrs A not sticking to the boundaries and her obtuseness in not realizing what she was doing, was also a feature of how other people reacted to her. For instance, in her anxiety to do the job well and please her boss, Mrs A would find herself asking her boss more and more questions about the task in hand and would get an increasingly sharp and irritated response from her. Similarly, her way of dealing with her sister, for example, in trying to get them to be close again, in fact had the opposite effect of driving the sister further away.

Now that Mrs A's difficulty with the punctual ending of the session made sense to him, the counsellor was no longer irritated by the way Mrs A accommodated, or more accurately, failed to accommodate to the time boundary of the session. He could now see her behaviour at the end of each session as a manifestation of some of her difficulties in managing close relationships. He waited until Mrs A next spoke of an unresolved encounter, this time concerning her boss and an unfinished project, and then said to her that he had noticed something similar happening in the counselling with him. He said that she did not seem to know how to finish the session with him but seemed compelled to try to prolong the session by checking on the time of the next session or asking him questions concerning the progress of the counselling.

Mrs A was initially taken aback by the counsellor's comment, and in a small and embarrassed tone of voice apologized for her behaviour and said she would make sure that in future she would not say anything once the counsellor had ended the session. The counsellor realized that Mrs A's response to his observation to her had turned it into a situation where he was telling her off for having done something wrong, for which she had to apologize. He further realized that this was her typical way of dealing with any conflict or disagreement in her relations with others. So he pointed this out to her, saying 'I am struck by how you have responded to what I have just said to you, as though I have been telling you off for something you have done wrong. This is exactly how you describe yourself responding to suggestions from senior staff at work...' (and here the counsellor quoted a couple of recent examples given by Mrs A). This time Mrs A was thoughtful, and then said she could see what the counsellor was getting at. She then started to talk about how uncomfortable she found the ending of the session, she felt shot down while in full flight, and in fact she now found herself getting anxious in the session as she realized the end of the session was approaching. The counsellor thought how Mrs A's description of how she felt about the end of the session reminded him of the little she had said concerning her mother's death, and it suddenly struck him how she had been avoiding this subject. He said to Mrs A that it had occurred to him that she might feel that the end of the session was like a death. Mrs A could see the obvious significance of the counsellor's words. After another pause she started to cry, and then spoke with much more feeling than previously about the circumstances of her mother's death.

In this example we can see how the way Mrs A accommodated to the setting revealed how she managed her life generally and relationships in particular. Pointing this out to the client was like holding up a mirror to her, showing her in the here and now how she was repeating a pattern in the room which went on in her relationships outside. The counsellor could only do this, however, when he had contained his initial feelings of irritation and annoyance, and been able to think about the meaning of Mrs A's difficulty in keeping to the time boundary of the session.

This example also illustrates a basic principle of psychoanalytic thinking, which Freud called the 'overdetermination' of meaning. This is the idea that no single or exhaustive meaning can ever be given to something, that any given situation can be interpreted in more than one way. So Mrs A's difficulty in ending the session was first seen as part of her pattern of not knowing how to bring an encounter to a satisfactory resolution. It then came to represent her difficulty in mourning her mother's death. In fact, as the counselling progressed, further meanings were given to the situation. It emerged that Mrs A tended to feel controlled in relationships, and would find ways of asserting her own control, often deviously. The counsellor was able to link this behaviour to her way of trying to prolong the session. The counsellor's impression that Mrs A was trying to cling on to him after he had ended the session also made sense when linked with her feeling of abandonment when her mother died, and how she could not come to terms with the fact that her mother was no longer there. Pointing out to Mrs A how she enacted these patterns in her manner of dealing with the end of each session had a powerful effect on her and helped her understand in an immediate and vivid way how she managed issues of closeness and loss in her relationships.

Here we can see how the counselling relationship between counsellor and client comes to take on a life and history of its own, and that many of the most significant events in this relationship concern how the client adapts to the setting. These shared events become points of reference and can be used as the basis for future understanding.

(c) The schedule is fixed

On one occasion a few weeks later Mrs A asked if she could change the time of the next session, as she had been asked by her boss to make a presentation to the whole team at that time. Now the counsellor was generally sympathetic to the demands of everyday life on his clients' schedule. However in this case he was aware that he felt under a lot of pressure to accede to Mrs A's request. When he thought about it, he realized that she had given him very little notice, although she usually seemed to know about having to do presentations a long time in advance as her boss was usually portrayed as a well-organized person. The counsellor decided to resist the pressure on him to agree right away to change this feature of the setting, that sessions should be at the same time each week, and chose instead to explore the meaning of Mrs A's request. He therefore said that, of course, he would consider Mrs A's request but he would like to find out more about it first. Mrs A then admitted that, in fact, the presentation had initially been made for another time, which would not have clashed with her counselling session, but on this occasion her boss had wanted to change the arranged time as she had some other engagement. The boss had therefore asked Mrs A whether she would mind changing the time of her presentation, which prompted Mrs A, always anxious to please her boss, to ask the counsellor to agree to a change in their schedule.

It was then clear to the counsellor that he should not agree to Mrs A's request, for he would then be letting her off the hook of her conflict over whether to please her boss or stand up for herself. By allowing her to pass over the decision to him, he would implicitly convey to her that she was not capable of managing her own conflict. Furthermore, by saying yes to her request he would be acting in the same way as Mrs A, that is as someone incapable of saying no. He therefore said to Mrs A that he thought it important to stick to the agreed time of their sessions, and pointed out to her that her request to him was actually a way of evading making her own decision about what to do with her boss. Mrs A at first looked disappointed, but then, after a pause, said she was actually relieved that the counsellor had said no, as she realized this was something she needed to sort out with her boss. Subsequently Mrs A told her boss that she could not make the changed time for the presentation. To her surprise her boss accepted this. This brought home to Mrs A how she had an expectation of how people would treat her, getting angry or retaliating if she said no to them, which often did not accord with reality.

Here is another example of an attempt to change one of the parameters of the setting revealing a typical pattern of behaviour on the client's part. By standing firm in the face of Mrs A's request the counsellor demonstrated that saying no was a manageable event, an experience the client was able to carry over into her dealings with people in the world.

This occurrence again became part of the shared history of the counselling. It brought Mrs A further along the way to acknowledging how she feared saying no to figures in authority, and this eventually led her to think about her mother, whom she also had tried to please all through her life.

(d) Breaks in the schedule and the counsellor keeping his personal life out of the counselling

The first holiday break in the counselling came after nearly three months. On the counsellor's return after a three-week absence Mrs A anxiously plied him with questions about his holiday. The counsellor felt under pressure to reply to her questions, as though it would be rude to withhold such innocuous information. However even though he could easily have answered her queries he felt it was more important to stick to his normal conduct, of not revealing details of his personal life, and try to find out what was making Mrs A so anxious. He therefore did not answer her questions but simply asked Mrs A what had stimulated her curiosity. Mrs A was initially angry, saying what was so terrible about asking the counsellor where he had gone on holiday? The counsellor commented that this was the first time Mrs A had been openly angry with him, and this made Mrs A stop and think. She then said that in fact she had been very anxious over the holiday break, and had had thoughts that something terrible might happen to the counsellor and that he might not return. She added that she had been very relieved when she had seen him at the beginning of the session, and now realized that she had covered up her anxiety and relief by asking him these questions. The counsellor made the obvious link to her mother's death, and commented that Mrs A was reacting to the break as though she believed the counsellor was not going to come back. He added that he thought that she had been angry with him for having taken a break, for interrupting the regular pattern of sessions and abandoning her over the holiday period, and this was why she had questioned him so persistently at the beginning of the session.

Mrs A was silent for a time, and then went on to say that she had suddenly remembered her first reaction to hearing the news that her mother had died. Her very first thought had been 'about bloody time too', as her mother's illness had been drawn out and she had been irritable and demanding with Mrs A. She had subsequently 'forgotten' this incident, as it disturbed her image of her mother as a model parent, as someone she felt she could never match. She was now beginning to acknowledge that in fact she had idealized her mother as a way of avoiding feeling any anger or disappointment towards her.

In this example the client's unusual behaviour, plying him with personal questions, was clearly linked to her experience of a break in the continuity of the sessions. The counsellor's attitude of not disclosing aspects of his own life can appear harsh, even perverse. What can be more natural than for the client to ask the counsellor where he went on holiday, and for the counsellor to reply? There has to be allowance for everyday politeness, and the counsellor had in fact responded to Mrs A's first question about whether he had had a good holiday. However by not answering her subsequent requests for more information the counsellor kept the focus on Mrs A and her anxieties about the break. This containing firmness on the counsellor's part, and his interpretation of her anger at his absence over the holiday, opened the way for Mrs A to get in touch with a memory of her anger towards her mother, a first step towards breaking down the idealization of her mother which had prevented her from recovering from her mother's death.

(e) There is normally no contact with third parties

The second holiday break also proved a difficult time for Mrs A, and soon after she restarted counselling she said that her husband was becoming increasingly worried about the effect of the counselling on her and would like to come and talk to the counsellor about whether the counselling was helping Mrs A. The counsellor replied that he was puzzled as to why she was making this request on her husband's behalf as he had told her in the initial session about the confidentiality of the counselling and that no third parties would be involved and it was clear that Mrs A had understood this. Mrs A at first reacted defensively, saying her husband was simply concerned about her and had the right to know about the counselling which was so powerfully affecting his wife. When the counsellor reminded her, however, that she sometimes complained that her husband wanted to know everything about her life, and that on occasions she had to keep things secret from him in order to protect her privacy, Mrs A acknowledged that she did feel pushed by her husband to pass on his request, even though she was not really very happy about it. This led Mrs A to reflect on her husband's intrusiveness about her life, and how hard she found it to insist on parts of her life being private.

The counsellor was also able to point out that Mrs A had been using the figure of her husband to voice her own doubts about the value of the counselling, and this led to Mrs A being able to speak of how distressing she found the breaks in the counselling, where she felt all the progress that had been made was lost. This led on to a valuable avenue for further exploration: why Mrs A felt she could not hold on to the good things about the counselling over the holiday break, and came back as though everything had been lost and she had to start again. Mrs A was able to link this to her mother's death, and began to see that this was a major reason for her inability to truly mourn her mother's death. She realized that she feared if she really accepted that her mother had died, all her good feelings for her mother and memories of happy times with her would die with her, and she would be left with nothing of value in her life.

In all of these examples the counsellor's ability to stand firm in the face of Mrs A's difficulties in accommodating to the various features of the setting allowed her underlying anxieties to be explored and understood. This attitude on the counsellor's part, of protecting the setting and using it as a set situation, gave Mrs A confidence in the counselling and enabled her to link her ways of dealing with the counselling setting to her ways of behaving and managing her relationships outside.

Summary

The setting in which psychodynamic counselling takes place comprises the following features: the spatial and temporal parameters, the various aspects of the professional relationship between counsellor and client, and the nature of the counsellor's conduct and attitude towards the client. Together these features establish the setting as a boundary which demarcates the site of counselling from the world outside. The setting also functions like a skin, holding together all the functions of the counsellor. The counsellor regards the establishment and maintenance of the setting as an essential part of the counselling, and strives to repair any breaches in its fabric. At the same time he regards some breaches as both inevitable and valuable, as they show how each client accommodates to the setting, and this accommodation will reveal the typical patterns and conflicts in the client's conduct and relationships with others.

Further reading

Barnes, F and Murdin, L (2001) *Values and Ethics in the Practice of Psychotherapy and Counselling*, London: Open University Press.

Bond, T (1993) *Standards and Ethics for Counselling in Action*, London: Sage.

British Association of Counselling and Psychotherapy (2009) 'Ethical Framework', which incorporates 'Ethical Framework for Good Practice in Counselling and Psychotherapy', available from the BACP website at www.bacp.co.uk.

Gray, A (1994) *The Therapeutic Frame*, London: Routledge.

Jacobs, M (1988) 'The importance of time and boundaries', Ch. 4 of *Psychodynamic Counselling in Action*, London: Sage.

Leiper, R and Maltby, M (2004) *The Psychodynamic Approach to Therapeutic Change*, London: Sage.

3

THEORY I: THE DEVELOPMENTAL POINT OF VIEW AND THE OEDIPUS COMPLEX

We have seen that psychodynamic counselling can be defined as a method of offering clients an experience of containment, that is finding both sanctuary from and meaning to their suffering. It is the setting which provides the most immediate form of sanctuary for the client. The setting also gives meaning to the client's behaviour in the way she accommodates to the setting. Psychoanalytic theory provides the psychodynamic counsellor with a framework which gives further meaning to the client's difficulties and problems, as well as her life in general.

Psychoanalytic theory is not, however, a unified field of ideas and concepts that fit neatly together. Although many psychoanalytic ideas still have their roots in Freud's theories, new psychoanalytic schools have developed with different and sometimes competing ways of thinking. Psychoanalytic theory as a whole is best thought of as a series of intellectual systems or conceptual frameworks which converge at numerous places and share a large number of basic assumptions, but also diverge in important ways. It is beyond the scope of this book to begin to demarcate the differences and divergences between these systems of thought. My aim is to present some basic theoretical ideas, derived primarily from Freud, Klein and Winnicott, and put them together into a coherent framework.

The purpose of theory

Before we come to look at psychoanalytic theory, we need first to ask ourselves whether we need theory at all. Clients sometimes express a hatred of being fitted into a theory, fearing that the counsellor will thereby rob them of their individuality. Counsellors also can approach psychoanalytic theory with suspicion, fearing it will take away their spontaneity and freedom to be themselves. These fears are not to be too lightly dismissed, as they point to a danger of mis-using theory as a kind of superior knowledge, a way of stamping one's authority onto a client deemed ignorant and inferior. Theory then becomes a form of received truth, whereby the counsellor is the one who knows and the client is the one in ignorance. In this way of thinking about theory the task of the counsellor is to impart this received knowledge to the client, like pouring water into an empty jug.

For overwhelmed or insecure counsellors – and all counsellors find themselves at sea with their clients from time to time – theory does have this seductive promise, of ridding one of uncertainties and partial understanding and substituting an illusion of total and complete knowledge. If theory is misused in this way, which is in effect an exercise in power, then there is indeed no room for the individuality of the client or the freedom of the counsellor.

But psychoanalytic theory has a quite different purpose for the psychodynamic counsellor. It is not there as a substitute for thought and creativity on the part of the counsellor but as its precondition. Just like the counselling setting provides a predictable boundary within which the unpredictability of the counselling relationship can develop, so theory provides a conceptual framework by means of which the counsellor can think for himself.

Theory does not replace experience, just as studying a map is not the same as walking over the terrain which it describes. What a map does is to provide bearings if you become lost, give a sketch of the surrounding area and its geography once you know where you are, and indicate the best route to take to one's destination and what is likely to be found on the way. There are also guidebooks which can give someone else's account of travelling where you are or want to go, and these can help you learn more from your travels. But a guidebook cannot determine what you will encounter when you travel yourself or whether you will experience things in a similar way to the writer of the guidebook. Maps and guidebooks are distillations of different perspectives and experiences put into a general and schematic framework, to be used by anyone who wants to orient themselves in terms of a universal schema. They provide a manageable context for the traveller to begin his own exploration.

A theoretical perspective on loss and attachment

We can see how theory can be used by returning to the case of Mrs A, who was described in the previous chapter. We have already seen how the counsellor linked the different parts of Mrs A's initial presentation into one overriding theme: her failure to mourn her mother's death. Over the course of the counselling the following picture emerged of how Mrs A dealt with the death of her mother.

Mrs A said she had always been close to her mother, in fact for much of her adult life she had spoken to her mother every day over the phone. Her mother's death did not come as a surprise as she had been ill for a long time, and near the end of her life had become increasingly frail. Mrs A spent a lot of time looking after her mother, who had lived on her own since Mrs A's father had died some years previously. The mother's last few weeks were spent in hospital, and Mrs A managed to visit her nearly every day. In a way, as she was able to acknowledge, her mother's death came as a relief as it meant her mother did not have to suffer any more and she, Mrs A, no longer had the shadow of her mother's impending death on the horizon.

For the first few days after her mother died, and for periods over the first few months, Mrs A said she felt numb. There were also occasional periods of great sadness, when she would cry, although crying brought her no relief. She withdrew from the world, seeking company only with her husband, and occasionally seeing her two daughters, who had their own families, or her sister. But after several months she gradually re-emerged from her overt feelings of grief and her life appeared to return to normal.

Yet below the surface things no longer felt the same. Mrs A described a constant state of restlessness, finding it hard to concentrate on one thing and tending to flit from one distraction to another. There was also a pervasive anxiety that something terrible would happen to her husband, her sister or her daughters. When this anxiety was at its height she would become phobic, for example avoiding crowded places and fearing to travel on public transport. She had bouts of uncontrollable crying, which would come on out of the blue. She felt her life had become pointless and she also felt intensely lonely.

Probably the worst reaction she described was being subjected to intrusive and disturbing thoughts, along the lines of 'you have been a bad daughter to your mother', or 'you have never done enough for your mother', even though she knew that she had actually been a dutiful daughter. She blamed herself for not having been attentive enough to her mother during her illness. She castigated herself for not having been present when her mother actually died, even though she knew perfectly well that this was due to circumstances beyond her control as she had been away at a work conference when the call from the hospital came, and she had rushed to the hospital as quickly as she could. It was mainly because of these thoughts that she had sought antidepressant medication and then counselling. The thoughts made her feel she was going mad.

Part of the pain of Mrs A's state of mind was that it made no sense to her, and this was one reason she felt she was going mad. By linking her experiences to her bereavement and her ways of coping with it, the counsellor gave her a framework in which her experiences were given a meaning. This framework was derived from a series of theoretical ideas on the nature of grief and loss as part of human development.

For example, Colin Murray Parkes, in his book *Bereavement: Studies of Grief in Adult Life* (1975), aimed to show how the pain of grief is a normal process. Parkes identified a series of stages which the normal pattern of grief passes through. In brief these are: a sense of alarm (shown for instance by restlessness), a period of searching for the dead person (accompanied by intense feelings of anxiety and pining), periods of mitigation or consolation (e.g. by a sense that the dead person is nearby or still around), anger with the dead person and guilt over their death. If the process of mourning is gone through, the bereaved person is not only able to recover, but can also gain a new identity, as they take in some positive or valuable aspects of the person they have lost. However those people who, for whatever reason, are not able to go through these stages would have a delayed or prolonged grief reaction. Parkes noted that in such cases, which could be called pathological grief reactions and may call for psychiatric intervention, the feelings of guilt or self-reproach were normally much more intense.

This schema helps us think about how Mrs A dealt with the death of her mother. Initially she appeared to go through a period of normal grief: a withdrawal from the world accompanied by preoccupying feelings of anxiety, sadness and guilt. Even her more intense and disturbing reactions, such as her bouts of uncontrollable crying and her intrusive and disturbing thoughts about her mother's death, could be considered features of a normal reaction to a devastating loss. However as time went on these manifestations of grief did not abate. Instead they took on a symptomatic quality, that is became fixed and debilitating states which did not allow for recovery or the rebuilding of her world.

Mrs A's counsellor used this kind of theoretical schema to provide a focus for the counselling: how to help Mrs A mourn the death of her mother. But such a schema does not help the counsellor understand *why* Mrs A's grief reaction was more pathological than normal.

One type of answer which can be given to this question is provided by a way of thinking called *attachment theory* (Holmes, 1994). This was developed by John Bowlby around a simple principle, which can be expressed as follows:

> What for convenience I am terming attachment theory is a way of conceptualizing the propensity of human beings to make strong affectional bonds to particular others and of explaining the many forms of emotional distress and personality disturbance, including anxiety, anger, depression, and emotional detachment, to which unwilling separation and loss give rise. (Bowlby, 1979, p. 127)

Bowlby traced an individual's pattern of attachment back to infancy and childhood, to their relationship to their parents or main carers. When babies and children feel confident of being loved and looked after they will develop what Bowlby called a pattern of secure attachment. This will show itself, for instance, in their developing belief in there being a 'secure base' from which they can be separate, but to which they can always return. An insecure pattern of attachment would be, for example, an 'anxious attachment', where children cling to their parents, as they are too frightened to let their parents out of their sight for too long. At the other extreme children who appear so self-sufficient that they seem not to need their parents are probably also manifesting a form of insecure attachment, but this time in an 'avoidant' form.

Both of these forms of insecure attachment were manifested by Mrs A. Her typical pattern of attachment was an anxious one, characterized by an overprotectiveness fuelled by a sense of guilt that she was not doing enough to preserve the relationship and fear that it would collapse. When this fear was at its most intense, she would seek to avoid relationships altogether, finding the outside world too frightening a place in which to venture out.

The developmental point of view

Both the investigations of normal and pathological grief and attachment theory depend on a developmental view of human growth. The pattern of attachment and the ways of coping with loss will be very different for an infant, an adolescent or an adult. Psychoanalytic theory has both influenced and been influenced by these ideas on mourning and attachment, and, like them, is based on a developmental point of view, that is, one which thinks of human growth in terms of the issues and tasks faced by the individual at any particular stage of development. Winnicott, for example, defined health as the 'maturity that belongs to the age of the individual' (Winnicott, 1986, p. 22). Each stage of the life cycle will involve the individual in the negotiation of particular tasks and challenges, and health can be determined by how successful or not this negotiation will be. The interplay of attachment, separation and loss runs like a thread throughout the whole life cycle, but will manifest itself in different forms or through different crises at each different stage. So, for instance, in infancy the management of the weaning process, by both the infant and parents or carers, is likely to set a pattern for the future negotiation of separation. Adolescents are faced with the loss of childhood and the necessary separation from parents, but this frees them to seek new attachments which match their growing physical, sexual and intellectual development. At each point in the life cycle – infancy, childhood, latency, adolescence, adulthood, midlife and old age – the individual will be faced by life tasks which will prove more or less difficult to negotiate (see Pincus and Dare, 1978, and Waddell, 1998 for an account of the life cycle).

From the developmental perspective life is not seen as easy. The person who does not find ordinary living at times difficult or even impossible is probably living a restricted or superficial life. Freud was very clear that psychoanalysis could not get rid of the ordinary problems of living. One of his definitions of the aim of psychoanalysis was to replace 'hysterical misery' with 'ordinary unhappiness' (Freud, 1895, p. 305). Psychoanalysis cannot therefore bring happiness, but it can aim to give or restore the opportunity for making life worthwhile, which for Freud meant 'the capacity to work and to love'. Winnicott's version of this is as follows:

> The life of a healthy individual is characterized by fears, conflicting feelings, doubts, frustrations, as much as by the positive features. The main thing is that the man or woman feels he or she is *living his or her own life,* taking responsibility for action or inaction, and able to take credit for success and blame for failure. In one language it can be said that the individual has emerged from dependence to independence, or to autonomy. (Winnicott, 1986, p. 27)

So in health too doubts, conflicts and the problems of living are still there to be contended with, and each individual will need to develop strategies and defences in order to try to master their anxiety and fears. Health is not then an absence of defences or of symptoms, but is characterized by flexibility and adaptation to the environment in their use. Winnicott puts it like this:

> A normal child *can* employ any or all of the devices which nature has provided in defence against anxiety and intolerable conflict. The devices employed (in health) are related to the kind of help that is available. Abnormality shows in a *limitation* and a *rigidity* in the child's capacity to employ symptoms, and a relative lack of relationship between the symptoms and what can be expected in the way of help. (Winnicott, 1964, p. 127)

Making sense of symptoms and the theory of repression

The developmental point of view offers a valuable perspective on an individual's behaviour and experience for it can be measured against a grid of normal social-psychological development. This developmental norm needs to take account of emotional factors as well as intellectual, cognitive and social ones so as to give a rounded picture of the developing individual. The limitation of the developmental perspective is that it tends to view an individual's behaviour and experience from the outside. For instance, Mrs A's depression could be usefully understood in developmental terms as a pathological grief reaction, and also as a consequence of insecure attachment, but it leaves out a picture of what might have been going on in her mind. What Freud aimed to do, and this has been the thrust of psychoanalytic theory, is to try to look at an individual from the inside, by constructing models of mental processes and the mind, and seeing how they both influence and are influenced by events and relationships in the external world.

Freud approached the subject of the make-up of an individual's mind by trying to find meaning in the behaviour and states of mind experienced by patients, and which appeared to be both senseless and pointless. In his *Introductory Lectures on Psychoanalysis*, delivered in 1915–16, he gave an example from one of his own patients, a 19-year-old girl, of an elaborate sleep ceremonial. This had developed in the last few years, and coincided with a change in the girl's attitude from being lively to being withdrawn and irritable, especially towards her mother. She was generally depressed, had became agoraphobic, and subject to indecisiveness and constant doubt. The focal point of her illness was a sleep-ceremonial, which she had to go through each night with her parents in order to get to sleep. Freud pointed out that everyone develops a kind of sleep-ceremonial, a particular ritualized way of going to sleep. Normally the parts of this ceremonial act like an adaptive symptom which serves its function, to manage the anxiety which can mark the transition from waking to sleep. But in this case not only were the aspects of the sleep-ceremonial rigidly performed and long drawn out, they seemed as much designed to prevent sleep as to foster it. The girl justified some of what she did by saying she needed absolute quiet in order to get to sleep. For instance anything that might be breakable, such as flowerpots and vases were put securely together on her writing table so that they might not fall over in the night and break. These had some link, if tenuous, to her need for quiet. But she also required that the door between her room and that of parents should stay half open, which she ensured by placing various objects in the open doorway. Here the rationale of needing quiet could no longer account for her demand. Finally her bed had to be made up in exactly the same way each night. For example her pillow at the top end of the bed could not touch the wooden back of her bedstead. Her eiderdown had to be shaken in a particular way so that most of the feathers were at the bottom end, which became very thick. These then had to be carefully smoothed out so no lumps remained. All of these precautions had to be checked over and over again and the rituals carried out exactly, with the result that one or two hours per night were spent by the girl and her parents before she, and the parents could be allowed to go to sleep (Freud, 1915, p. 265).

Freud's approach to these manifestations of strange behaviour was to find a context which would provide an overall meaning. The whole scenario, involving an adolescent girl's bedroom and its relation to her parents' bedroom, already suggested a sexual theme to him. The details of this sexual scenario and the more particular meaning of the aspects of her ceremonial became clearer in the analysis he conducted with the girl. Freud looked for the meaning of the girl's behaviour from two sources. One was from what might be called general cultural or symbolic knowledge. So he interpreted the girl's fear of vases or flowerpots being broken during the night as a sexual fear. This interpretation was based on an understanding of symbolic language, in which a vase can represent the female genitals, supported by a knowledge of everyday cultural practices, for instance the common practice in Europe of breaking a vessel or plate at betrothal ceremonies.

The other source of meaning for Freud, the one which he always regarded as the primary one, was from the patient herself, her memories and associations which provided a personal meaning to the symptoms. So, regarding the fear of breaking flowerpots and vases, the girl remembered as a child that she had fallen down while carrying a glass or china vase and had cut her finger which bled profusely. When she grew up and came to know the facts about sexual intercourse she developed the anxious idea that on her wedding night she would not bleed and therefore fail to show she was a virgin. Freud then put these symbolic and personal meanings together to argue that the parts of the sleep-ceremonial acted as a whole series of precautions designed to banish any representations of female sexuality and sexual intercourse from the girl's bedroom.

The girl found out the central meaning of the ceremonial herself when she suddenly remembered the meaning of the rule that the pillow must not touch the back of the bedstead. She said the pillow had always been a woman to her and the upright wooden back a man. Thus, said Freud she wanted by magic to keep the man and woman apart, that is to separate her parents from each other. In her earlier years she had suffered from night terrors, which were only alleviated when the door between her nursery and her parents' bedroom was kept open, and she had often managed to sleep in her parents' bed between them. Shaking the eiderdown so that it had a lump at one end, and then smoothing the lump over could be easily linked to her fear that her mother might become pregnant, as she had in fact feared for years that her parents wanted another child.

In following through these lines of analysis Freud came to the conclusion that the sleep-ceremonial did not have a single purpose but rather performed two different functions at the same time. He argued that 'the rules laid down by the ceremonial reproduced the patient's sexual wishes at one point positively, and at another negatively – in part they represented them, but in part they served as a defence against them' (Freud, 1915, p. 269). So, for instance, the prohibition on the pillow and bedstead touching each other served as a defence against the idea of sexual intercourse, but was also a representation of it. In the ritual with the eiderdown the representation and then repudiation of pregnancy were symbolized by the two different parts of the ritual (creating the lump of feathers and then smoothing them out). Symptoms, then, are 'overdetermined', that is, they have more than one meaning.

Not only each individual symptom but the girl's illness as a whole can be seen to have this dual meaning of being both a repudiation and also an enactment of sexual ideas which the girl found unaccept-able. On the one hand her illness could be seen as a retreat from an acknowledgement of her sexual body, a flight back into latency or childhood when she could be once again protected by her parents from any knowledge of sexuality. But her illness was also a cov-ert way of dramatizing her sexual feelings, which were primarily directed, as Freud discovered, towards her father, towards whom she had an 'erotic attachment' dating back to her childhood. Freud remarked dryly on this hidden purpose of her symptoms:

> The conclusion she herself drew was that she could not marry as long as she was so ill. We, however, may suspect that she had become so ill in order not to have to marry and in order to remain with her father. (Freud, 1915, p. 273)

Such patients, said Freud, can be seen as:

> ... 'fixated' to a particular portion of their past, as though they could not manage to free themselves from it and were for that reason alienated from the present and the future. They then remained lodged in their illness in the sort of way in which in earlier days people retreated into a monastery in order to bear the burden there of their ill-fated lives. (Freud, 1915, p. 273)

Freud's theorizing was directed at finding meaning and purpose in the signs and symptoms of psychological distress. He saw them as functioning as a form of *defence,* a way of warding off *anxiety,* caused by mental pain and conflict, which would arise if certain unaccept-able feelings, thoughts and impulses were allowed free rein. For Freud's patient, her symptoms served to defend her against the anx-iety generated by her sexual feelings and thoughts, and by her over-all adolescent conflict of whether to remain a child or grow up into an adult. Her elaborate series of symptoms were a way of binding her anxiety, tying it down to a series of behaviours which although bizarre and burdensome gave her some sense of being in control.

The primary form of defence investigated by Freud was the mech-anism of *repression,* the process by which the unacceptable feelings, thoughts and impulses which generate anxiety are pushed out of the conscious mind and into a special region of the mind Freud called the *unconscious.* However repression is only partially success-ful. What has been pushed out of consciousness always strives to find a means of expression, which, said Freud, it does by presenting itself to the conscious mind in a disguised form. In Freud's patient the repressed sexual feelings and thoughts did find expression in her sleep-ceremonial, but as a kind of subterranean current. This is what Freud called 'the return of the repressed'. We never succeed in banishing those parts of ourselves which we find unacceptable, and every attempt to push them away, to repress them, only results in their return in a disguised and much more powerful form. The task of the analyst, then, is to retrace the steps of this repression, to uncover the repressed ideas, and then to discover from which part of the patient's past history the need for repression arose.

Although Freud took repression as an exemplar of how defences work, he identified other mechanisms of defence against anxiety and conflict. In the case of the girl with the sleep-ceremonial, for instance, she *displaced* her fear of sexuality onto objects which seemed to have nothing to do with what she feared, namely vases and flowerpots. When the object of the displacement is another person, this form of defence is called *projection*. So, for example, a person who wishes to rid themselves of unacceptable sexual thoughts or wishes might project them into someone else, and then experience that other person as though they were displaying the disowned and repudiated sexual thoughts and wishes. In this way the person can avoid recognizing and taking responsibility for their own state of mind by locating it in someone else.

In the case of Mrs A the feeling she found least acceptable was her anger, and the thoughts associated with it, and this feeling was subject to repression. However we can see that repression was not the only mechanism of defence employed. Mrs A *displaced* her anger with her mother onto other people, notably her boss, and so was often unreasonably angry with some of the things her boss did. This displacement was also a form of *projection* in that she disowned her own anger and located it in her boss. She *idealized* her mother as another way of keeping any thoughts of anger at bay. Critical thoughts she might have had against her mother were *turned round against herself* in the form of self-blaming intrusive thoughts (see Malan, 1979, and Brown and Peddar, 1979 for a fuller account of mechanisms of defence).

As well as making use of specific mechanisms of defence, one can also identify a typical defensive structure or system for an individual. In Freud's example the girl displayed both *obsessional* defences, the whole series of rituals and ceremonials which had to be meticulously followed through in order to prevent her from acting on her hidden feelings, and *phobic* ones, such as agoraphobia which restricted her freedom of movement to a minimum and so lessened the chance of an unexpected sexual encounter. Mrs A also used phobic defences, for example, her fear of travelling, but her more typical form of defence was an *hysterical* one (e.g. her uncontrollable outbursts of crying). The hysterical defence has its origin in a profound sense of worthlessness, a conviction that no one will take you seriously unless you force them to take notice of you by an exaggerated and dramatic display of feelings (Rycroft, 1988).

The ego, identification with the object and the structure of depression

In trying to make sense of Mrs A's depression, we have so far concentrated on the feelings, thoughts and impulses which have been defended against. Indeed, depression itself can be regarded as a form of defence, a defence against liveliness which is seen as threatening. We can then go on to wonder: if symptoms, indeed psychological illness itself is seen as a form of defence – a defence which has outlived its usefulness and taken control over the personality – who or what is the agent of these defensive operations?

Freud's answer to this question was to identify an agency in the mind he called the *ego* (the German term he used was 'das Ich', the 'I') which organizes the various mental processes, and in particular sets in motion the various mechanisms of defence. He saw the ego as the link between the other parts of the mind, on the one hand feelings and impulses straining to find expression (a part of the mind he called the 'id'), and on the other hand the moral strictures and ideals inculcated as a child from society as a whole and one's parents in particular (which he called the 'superego'). The ego also mediates the requirements of the external world, to which the mind must adapt.

Freud came to pay increasing attention to how the ego was formed, and he turned to an investigation of depression, or melancholia as he termed it, to find an answer. He began by comparing the person in mourning with the melancholic. Both are sad and dejected, both are withdrawn from the world and act as though they have suffered a traumatic loss. However there is a fundamental difference between the two. Mourning is the result of a bereavement, the loss of another person, whereas for the melancholic what is lost is a belief in himself. Freud put it like this:

The melancholic displays something else beside which is lacking in mourning – an extraordinary diminution in his self-regard, an impoverishment of his ego on a grand scale. In mourning it is the world which has become poor and empty; in melancholia it is the ego itself. (Freud, 1917, p. 246)

Freud explained this impoverishment of the ego in melancholia as the loss of the integrity of the ego. The ego becomes split into two parts, and we see in the melancholic 'how in him one part of the ego sets itself over against the other, judges it critically, and, as it were, takes it as its own object' (Freud, 1917, p. 247). We have seen this with Mrs A, in her self-accusations that she had not been a good daughter to her mother.

Freud then asks how this division of the ego, into a critical and an abased part, comes about.

If one listens patiently to a melancholic's many and various self-accusations, one cannot in the end avoid the impression that often the most violent of them are hardly at all applicable to the patient himself, but that with insignificant modifications they do fit someone else, someone whom the patient loves or has loved or should love...So we find the key to the clinical picture: we perceive that the self-reproaches are reproaches against a loved object which have been shifted away from it on the patient's own ego. (Freud, 1917, p. 248)

Freud reconstructed this process as follows. At one time there was a real attachment to a person, but then, for whatever reason, this relationship was shattered. The result, however, was not the normal one of withdrawal of attachment and involvement from the love-object and displacement onto a new one. Instead Freud imagined a withdrawal of this psychic energy away from the figure in the external world and into the ego. This turning in on itself by the ego establishes a division within the ego. One part *identifies* with the abandoned person (called an 'object' in psychoanalytic discourse to indicate it is the object or recipient of the individual's feelings or impulses). This identification entails a modification of the ego on the model of the abandoned object; Freud's metaphor to describe this process was that 'the shadow of the object fell upon the ego' (Freud, 1917, p. 249). The other part of the ego then treats this newly formed part of the ego as if it was the abandoned object itself, and berates and attacks it as the cause of all its misery. And so, 'in this way an object-loss was transformed into an ego-loss and the conflict between the ego and the loved person into a cleavage between the critical agency of the ego and the ego as altered by identification' (ibid.). Freud thus envisaged the ego like an archaeological site, layered with the remains of former loved and hated objects.

We can see an example of the alteration of the ego through identification with an object in Mrs A's relationship with her mother. Mrs A had always been close to her mother, they would always confide in each other, and Mrs A found her mother to be both supportive and generous. However there was another dimension to the relationship, one which was more difficult for Mrs A to explore. She recalled her mother as having periods of sadness or depression. Although she most clearly remembered these feelings of her mother's at the time of her father's death, during the counselling she started to recall that during her adolescence she would sometimes come upon her mother crying for no reason. She had never understood the reason for her mother's sadness and had never wanted to find out.

As well as finding her mother a pathetic figure, she also at times found her to be a critical and angry one. She remembered with considerable shame being stung by her mother's sharp criticism of her as an adolescent. Her mother's disappointment in her would probably be for something trivial, but Mrs A, so dependent on her mother for her self-esteem, experienced such criticisms as crushing.

So alongside an identification with her mother as a positive and nurturing figure, an identification which enriched her ego, there was also an identification with her mother as both an abject and contemptible object and also as a cruelly attacking one. In the process of this identification Mrs A's ego became split, with one part cruelly attacking the other part as pathetic and worthless, just as her own mother had treated her.

However the mother with whom Mrs A identified seemed to be a far harsher and crueller figure, as well as a more debased one than her mother ever was in real life. It was as though Mrs A was identifying not only with her real mother, but also with some kind of fantasy figure constructed within her own mind. How could this be accounted for?

The Oedipus complex

From the beginning of his career as a psychotherapist Freud had been trying to find a way to account for the development of symptoms and mental illness or distress in his patients. His first idea was that some external trauma must always be to blame, some overwhelming impingement from outside with which the psychic apparatus could not deal, and therefore had to resort to massive repression. Since he actually encountered instances of sexual abuse among some of his patients, he initially put this forward as the necessary condition for the development of neurosis or mental distress. But Freud soon found this explanation insufficient, as some people became ill with no obvious external trauma, and some people who had suffered a massive trauma stayed healthy. The trouble with focusing exclusively on the idea of an external trauma was that it ignored the contribution of the other parts or agencies of the mind. Freud always took account of the crucial importance of external events, but he came to see that an internal drama needed to be understood as well in order to give a more satisfying account of the development of symptoms.

Freud came to the idea of a particular 'complex', a pattern of relationships with its origin in the child's place in the family, which he saw as a critical point in the development of the individual. Failure to successfully negotiate this critical phase would result in a need for more repression and therefore make more likely the formation of symptoms. This constellation of relationships was both external, to do with the child's relationship with his or her actual parents, and internal, as this relationship pattern then became internalized to form part of the structure of the mind. Freud called this constellation of relationships the Oedipus complex.

The Oedipus complex refers to the pattern of relationships between the child and his or her parents which shape the child's emotional, psychological and sexual development. It is a way of thinking about how the child navigates its way through the complexities of needing to identify with his or her parents, that is becoming like them, while also separating from them, that is being different from them. It is about the way the child makes sense of the difference between the sexes and between the generations.

Freud thought the child negotiates the Oedipus complex in several stages. For the male child, his first love-object is his mother, a love which starts with him feeding at her breast. But, said Freud, while the little boy loves his mother and desires to be close to her, he identifies and wishes to be like his father. For a time these two relationships, love for mother and identification with father proceed side by side. But at some point, perhaps due to an increase of intensity in his love for his mother, the boy comes up against a barrier. He is forced to acknowledge a reality of both generation and gender: that it is his father who has a prior claim on his mother, and stands in the way of him becoming too close, or acting like a lover to his mother. In the boy's mind the father has now become an obstacle, a rival for his mother's love. This development marks the beginning of the Oedipus complex. The boy's identification with his father now takes on a hostile colouring. Together with his continuing admiration and love for his father as the person he wishes to emulate, the boy now wishes to get rid of his father in order take his place and have his mother to himself. From now on the little boy's relationship with his father is ambivalent.

This, then, is what Freud called the simple form of the Oedipus complex, so called because it is based on Sophocles' story of Oedipus, who killed his father and married his mother. Freud initially saw the little girl following a similar path, having to negotiate taking her father as a love-object, and then encountering her mother as both an object of identification and as a rival for the father's affection. However he then realized that the situation of the little boy and girl is not symmetrical, as both have the experience of the mother's love and attention from the beginning, expressed above all in the feeding relationship to the breast. The little boy continues taking his mother as his love-object, whereas the little girl has to transfer her love for her mother onto the figure of her father before she enters the simple form of the Oedipus complex. For both the little boy and the little girl, then, this initial relationship with the mother plays a vital part in their readiness to enter into the Oedipus complex.

However the 'simple' form of the Oedipus complex was a notional one for Freud, for in his view little boys and girls do not have a fixed gender identity. In his words they are 'psychically bisexual', that is able to take on the behaviour and experience of both genders. The little boy, as well as loving his mother and having his father as both rival and object of identification, also loves his father and identifies with his mother. In a complementary way the little girl takes each parent as both love-object and object of identification. So, for Freud, each child has to negotiate this constellation of 'object-choices and identifications', this bisection of desire ('I love my mother/ father') with identity ('I am like my mother/father') which forms the Oedipus complex in its 'complete' form. There is no predetermined outcome, as the child will go through the range of Oedipal feelings (love, hate, jealousy, affection) and identifications with each parent before coming to a more fixed constellation. The way the Oedipus complex is negotiated will establish a template of relationships and states of mind which will serve as a backdrop to all of the growing child's future dealings with other people (Freud, 1923).

There is an implicit idea of successful or unsuccessful negotiation of the Oedipus complex. This has led some practitioners (more so in the past than today) to use the Oedipus complex in a reductionist and moralistic way as a justification of their own prejudices, notably in equating the successful outcome with the finding of a 'correct' love-object, that is a heterosexual one. However Freud considered the Oedipus complex as a much more subtle instrument, where it is the range of identifications and the quality of relationships rather than the simple choice of object which determines how successfully the Oedipus complex has been negotiated. For Freud a mark of the successful negotiation of the Oedipus complex is a person's ability to become independent of their parents. Much of the impetus for this comes from the child's inevitable frustration of his Oedipal feelings (e.g. the little boy has to give up his possessive love for his mother as he is too small to really compete with father for her love), which pushes him or her to find satisfaction in other relationships. The drive and intensity of Oedipal feelings, once turned away from the frustrating parental figures, is then available to be used in other areas of the child's life, for example, in intellectual or artistic development (Freud called this process 'sublimation', which he saw as an essential part of an individual's development). Inhibition and impotence, both in relationships and achievements in life are signs of a person who has remained stuck at some point in their negotiation of the Oedipus complex.

For example Freud traced sexual impotence in men back to a failure to negotiate the vicissitudes of love and sexual desire. The impotent man will, typically, have a relationship with a woman he admires and for whom he feels affection, but only be able to have sex with a woman he despises. As a child, Freud argued, such a man had to disown his desire for his loved mother for fear of punishment by the father. But he was never able to find a way of reuniting his desire for his mother with his love for her. Instead sexual desire became repressed and displaced onto other female figures, who were despised as Oedipally forbidden objects. In such a way he could preserve an ideal and sexually purified image of his mother as someone he could love and hold in high esteem without incurring his father's rivalry, and any future wife or partner would be closely modelled on this idealized figure. But the cost of this split, which is a failure to tolerate ambivalence in his feelings towards his mother (and father) is high. For such men: 'Where they love they do not desire and where they desire they cannot love' (Freud, 1910, p. 183). The lesson Freud drew from such examples was that 'anyone who is to be really free and happy in love must have surmounted his respect for women and have come to terms with the idea of incest with his mother or sister' (Freud, 1910, p. 186).

Freud saw the Oedipus complex as a phase through which each individual passes in his or her psychical and emotional development, roughly spanning the period between childhood and latency, around the ages of three to six years. This is the time when the child starts to move away from the parents, starts school and discovers the world outside the family. Oedipal feelings and thoughts serve as a backdrop to all of our significant relationships and are reactivated with particular intensity around critical developmental periods such as adolescence, leaving home, finding a partner or the birth of a first baby. The Oedipus complex plays a crucial role in determining the make-up of the agencies of the mind, for the superego is formed out of the internalization of the original parental prohibition against incest. The outcome of this phase will be crucially affected by external realities and events. For example a parent who is in reality harsh and persecuting is more likely to turn the child's superego into a cruelly attacking part of the mind. Or a parent who dies or leaves when Oedipal feelings are at their height is likely to leave the child believing in the murderousness of their hatred or the deadliness of their love.

The Oedipus complex helps in understanding the devastating effect of sexual abuse within the family. The damage to the child is not only that of physical and sexual violation, often accompanied by actual or threatened violence, together with the betrayal of trust and the fact that the child is often not believed. It is compounded by the collapse of the distinction between wish and deed, symbolic and actual. The child no longer has the chance to come to terms with what Freud called the 'idea of incest', for incest is no longer an idea but a reality imposed by others to which the child has had to submit. The whole symbolic register in which the Oedipus complex takes place – where the child is free to play the different roles of lover, rival, accomplice and so on – becomes out of bounds. Negotiation of the Oedipus complex is foreclosed, as Oedipal thoughts and desires become too disturbing or frightening to tolerate (Bollas, 1989).

The phenomenon of sexual abuse shows that the child's Oedipal feelings towards its parents has to be placed in the context of the parents' Oedipal feelings towards their child. Although developmentally the intensity of feelings and thoughts that belong to the Oedipus complex reach their peak during the Oedipal phase, one can speak of an Oedipal schema as being in existence from the time the child is conceived and then born. Each baby will be born into a pattern of relationships established by the parents, and other significant family members. In particular the child will come up against the range of object choices and identifications in the unconscious of each parent, which will largely determine how they will experience the newly born baby. In cases of actual sexual abuse, for example, the abused child may be experienced by the abusing parent (and/or by the non-abusing parent) as a seductive lover, as though it was the child whose sexual desire initiated the abuse. In such an example the parents, as well as the child will be unable to differentiate between child-like affection and adult sexual desire (what Ferenczi, 1985, called 'the confusion of tongues between the child and the adults'). Even when Oedipal feelings and desires are not acted out, the place the child occupies in the mind of the parents will still play a significant part in the child's Oedipal development. So, for instance, a mother who conveys to a little boy that his father is an unreliable or a dangerous figure is likely to make it more difficult for the boy to identify with him, unlike the mother who relates to the father as a loveable and admirable man.

As well as being a developmental concept, the Oedipus complex can also be seen as a structural concept in the sense that it constitutes all relationships as essentially triadic. There is no such thing as an exclusively dyadic or dual relationship, for instance between a mother and infant, for there is always the idea, if not the actual presence, of the father. It is a mark of the person who has not successfully negotiated the Oedipus complex that they find particular difficulties in the triangular nature of relationships, for example, being prone to intense jealousy of their partner if they come into too close contact with other people (Tame, 1996).

Such was the case with Mrs A whose marriage was at times like the 'babes in the wood', in which she and her husband clung to each other in the face of a rather hostile and confusing world. It soon became clear that this was largely because both Mrs A and her husband found jealousy particularly hard to cope with, and so avoided as far as possible any situation involving other people which might provoke such a reaction.

The Oedipal origins of this fear of jealousy became evident as Mrs A explored her relationship to her mother in more depth. Initially she was puzzled as to why she and her mother would have reason to be angry with, or even hate each other, as they normally got on so well together, and had a relationship based on mutual affection and respect. However Mrs A did acknowledge that she and her mother had been less close to each other around the time of her marriage. Her mother had never said anything, but did manage to convey that she felt that Mrs A's husband was not really good enough for her. In fact, when she thought about it. Mrs A was forced to concede that her mother had never been very complimentary about any of her boyfriends, and in fact had never seemed too upset when these relationships came to an end. Mrs A's mother was only able to accept Mrs A's husband when she realized that her daughter's marriage would not threaten the intimate relationship she had with her daughter, which continued more or less as before.

As Mrs A talked more about her mother, the counsellor realized that, while he now had a rounded and developed picture of Mrs A's mother in his mind, he had virtually no sense of Mrs A's father, and he said this to Mrs A, observing that Mrs A hardly ever talked about him. Her immediate reply was 'there's nothing much to say about him'. He was several years older than her mother, a rather distant figure, who worked as a civil servant and often did not come home until late in the evening because of meetings at work. He was never particularly interested in the children, seeing them as his wife's province. Mrs A had few memories of her father playing with her or her sister. When he died she had little feeling, beyond a generalized feeling of sadness and regret.

In a later session, however, while speaking of her sister, Mrs A mentioned that her sister has always been jealous of her, as she had been her father's favourite. This remark surprised the counsellor, as it did not fit in with what Mrs A had said previously about her father, and he commented on this. Mrs A then began to speak of a time when she had been close to her father, around the age of eight or so. There were trips to the cinema or outings with him, sometimes with mother and sister, but sometimes on her own with him. Then, suddenly, the trips with just herself and her father came to an end. Mrs A could not remember why these had stopped, although she did have some vague memories of having been hurt by the change in her father's attitude towards her, which she put down to her father's irritability and preoccupation with his work.

Then she started to remember two things about her mother, at around the same period in her childhood. One was that she and her mother became very close. Mother used to gossip and confide in her about her life and her friends. In particular she remembered mother talking about her father, and describing her disappointment in him as a husband, how he never paid her enough attention and, although a good worker, was really 'useless' in other areas of their life. She also remembered having occasional temper tantrums with her mother, which she had never been able to understand. These persisted until her adolescence, when they reached a peak, and then subsided.

The counsellor was then able to put the various pieces together into the following reconstruction, which he offered to Mrs A. He said that her closeness to her father had brought about a conflict for her. It provoked jealousy in both her sister and her mother. In addition it led to her mother denigrating her father, which Mrs A probably experienced as an Oedipal prohibition against further involvement with him. This led her to turn away from her father (a move which might well have also been motivated by her own inevitable moving away from her father as she became more interested in her peers, and perhaps reinforced by the father's fear of getting too close to his daughter). Although this resulted in a close and in many ways satisfying relationship with her mother, it did have a further consequence: Mrs A lost faith in herself as a sexually attractive girl and woman. Her desirability did not get the confirmation it needed from her father, whom Mrs A felt had rejected her, nor from her mother who did not present her father as a desirable figure who could validate her attractiveness. This was the reason for her angry outbursts against her mother, her sense that her mother had deprived her of a satisfactory relationship with her father.

Mrs A's initial response to this interpretation, after a long silence in which she was clearly digesting what the counsellor had said, was to suddenly remember a recurring dream she had had as a child, which had always frightened and puzzled her. She used to dream that 'she had been buried alive in a coffin under the ground. The coffin was in fact quite big for her, giving her room to move about in, and this was because it was not her coffin but her mother's'. She used to think the dream was about her mother's death, something she had always feared. But now she could see that the dream also expressed some idea of being trapped inside her mother and unable to get out to the world outside. Mrs A went on to say that what the counsellor had said made sense of how she related to her husband, in terms of the restricted and overprotective nature of their marriage, as well as to her own daughters. For example she had never felt comfortable in the presence of her daughters' husbands, and now she could see that she was in fact jealous of the closeness they had with her daughters. She could trace these feelings back to her relationship with her mother, and her difficulty in accepting her ambivalent feelings for her mother; loving her but also hating her as an Oedipal rival who, Mrs A felt, had kept her imprisoned in an over-close bond with her instead of encouraging her to find relationships in the world outside.

The counsellor's reconstruction of Mrs A's childhood relationship with her mother and father, which went through a number of modifications over the course of the counselling as Mrs A added more memories and reflections, helped Mrs A understand the difficulties she was having in mourning her mother's death. In particular, the strength of her ambivalent feelings towards her mother (and her father) became both more evident and more acceptable to her, and helped her gradually and painfully come more to terms with her bereavement.

The concept of the Oedipus complex provides the answer to the question we posed at the end of the previous section: why was Mrs A's mother, as incorporated into her ego, a harsher and more abject figure than her actual mother? We can now see that the mother who became part of Mrs A's ego was the Oedipal mother. As such she was an angry and rivalrous figure, attacking Mrs A for wishing to be desirable to her father and to other men. She was also a despised figure, rendered pathetic by Mrs A's wish to triumph over her mother and remove her as an obstacle to her relationships with men.

The Oedipus complex deepens our understanding of both external and internal reality. It illuminates the way the client experiences her close and intimate relationships, and how they are modelled on the family dynamics of childhood. At the same time it draws a picture of the mind in terms of the Oedipal figures and their relationships with each other. Such figures, and their attributes and qualities came to be called 'internal objects' in psychoanalytic language, and it is to an investigation of these that we now turn.

(A summary of this chapter and suggestions for further reading can be found at the end of Chapter 4.)

4

Theory II: The Internal World and the Depressive and Paranoid-Schizoid Modes of Experience

Internal objects and the internal world

We have seen that the Oedipus complex describes a drama which is not only external, to do with the child's relationships with family members, but also an internal one about a series of Oedipal figures in the mind, who have different kinds of relationships with each other. Melanie Klein, and those influenced by her thinking, expanded this idea of figures in the mind into the idea of an internal world, as a counterpart to the external world. She envisaged this internal world as made up of parts of the ego and parts of external objects which have been taken inside, and which are in constant interaction with each other. She thought the content and boundaries of the internal world were established early in life, in infancy, although subject to modification and development later on. For the baby the internal world starts off as the internalization of aspects of his or her parents.

> The baby, having incorporated his parents, feels them to be live people inside his body in the concrete way in which deep unconscious phantasies are experienced – they are, in his mind, 'internal' or 'inner' objects, as I have termed them. Thus an inner world is being built up in the child's unconscious mind, corresponding to his actual experiences and the impressions he gains from people and the external world, and yet altered by his own phantasies and impulses. (Klein, 1940, p. 148)

Klein envisaged the internal object, for example, the internal mother, as a 'double' of the external one, but a double altered by the individual's phantasies and state of mind when the external object is internalized. Once incorporated the internal mother can no longer be perceived in the way the mother in the world outside can be studied and observed. So the infant or child has to look to the real mother, not only to understand the mother as she is in the world, but also to comprehend better his own internal mother. As Klein puts it, 'the visible mother thus provides continuous proofs of what the "internal" mother is like, whether she is loving or angry, helpful or revengeful' (Klein, 1940, p. 149). For example, if the child is angry with the mother, the mother's ability to withstand the child's rage without collapsing or retaliating will reassure the child that his loved mother, inside as well as outside, is not injured by his anger towards her.

We can illustrate the concepts of internal world, internal objects and unconscious phantasies by looking at one area of experience, eating. Winnicott, who was a paediatrician as well as a psychoanalyst and who encountered many instances of babies with feeding difficulties, used the idea of unconscious phantasies to explore the infant's experience of appetite.

Winnicott saw a progression from a simple to a more elaborate level of experience. At its most basic, the appetite of the infant is simply the recognition of both the need and the pleasure involved in taking things, especially food into the mouth. Winnicott imagined if the infant could speak he might put it like this: 'I want to suck, eat, bite. I enjoy sucking, eating, biting. I feel satisfied after sucking, eating, biting' (Winnicott, 1936, p. 34).

Next comes an elaboration of the simple function of eating to the beginning of thoughts and the imagining of events and stories about the food. In the imagined words of an infant: 'When hungry I think of food, when I eat I think of taking food in. I think of what I like to keep inside, and I think of what I want to be rid of and think of getting rid of it' (ibid.). Here we can see the development of primitive phantasies associated with appetite, and an appreciation of the difference between inner and outer.

Then comes what Winnicott described as a more sophisticated linking up of these phantasies with the idea of an inner world. This involves a deepening and an elaboration of the notion of what happens inside oneself, together with ideas of the state of the inside of the source of supply, namely the mother's body. 'I also think of what happens at the source of supply. When very hungry I think of robbing and even of destroying the source of supply and I then feel bad about what I have inside me and I think of means of getting it out of me, as quickly as possible and as completely as possible' (ibid.). The phantasies have now become more sophisticated, involving a relationship, however crude, with the mother's body (the source of supply), and based around primitive ideas of robbery, destruction and evacuation.

Winnicott observed that the infant and child tends to place the happenings of phantasies inside and to identify them with physical events inside the body.

> Children will often give an account of their inner world, when asked about their inner discomforts. One child says there is a war going on inside between Spaniards and English who fight with swords. Another recounts a fantasy of little people sitting round a table in his stomach, waiting for the food to be passed down. A little boy of four said he could hear little men knocking their plates about after he had eaten. Another said that there was a row of children sitting on a fence inside mother, and a birth occurs when father goes in and knocks one off with a crowbar. (Winnicott, 1936, p. 35)

It is what Winnicott called the limitless elaboration of such phantasies that constitutes the inner world. It functions as a backdrop to our thoughts and emotions, like a kind of moving scenery in a theatre which gives colour and atmosphere to the events happening on stage. Winnicott noted that the inner world may be kept inactive when feared, taking away some of the richness of our experience. In illness it may get over-controlled, or some of its elements may take control over the individual.

Winnicott gave an example of this in a girl of seven, who since the age of two had habitually scratched her genitals so that they were constantly inflamed and sore. In her consultation with Winnicott, the girl was eager to tell him of bad dreams which she could only keep away by keeping her eyes open. It was clear, Winnicott observed that she not only had anxiety dreams but visual hallucinations, partly awful and partly beautiful. Her happiness, she said, was to find enough niceness in the things she saw to balance out the nastiness. The chief thing was, she saw brown things coming out of holes, and she took these brown creatures in with her food. 'You see I'm very fond of liver and sausages and that's why they're brown mostly' (Winnicott, 1936, p. 37).

Winnicott's understanding of the girl's difficulties was that they were the expression of an internal drama. He postulated that for her eating involved the phantasy, constantly lived out that 'she had eaten good and bad people, and bits of people, and that according to the love and hate involved she has been enriched and burdened respectively with intensely sweet or terrifyingly grotesque objects in her inner world' (ibid.). She located the bad creatures in her genitals and was compelled to try and scratch them out.

Here we can see how an apparently senseless piece of compulsive behaviour, the little girl's constant scratching at her genitals, made sense when seen as the expression of a battle between objects in her internal world. The following example shows how a similar kind of internal drama can be played out in eating disorders in adults, and how the counsellor used the concept of an internal world to help the client make sense of her experience.

Ms B, a woman in her late twenties, referred herself to a counselling agency for help with an eating disorder. She was seen for weekly counselling of one year by a female counsellor. It soon became clear that Ms B's life was split into two parts. On the surface she led a successful and rewarding life. She had a good job as a teacher and was in fact, in line for promotion. She had a long-standing relationship with her boyfriend, and they had started to make plans to marry and have children. She had a busy social life and a number of close friends. However Ms B also had another life, a secret one dominated by bulimia, where she felt in the grip of its rigid and compulsive regime of binge eating followed by vomiting. This eating pattern had begun in her teens and continued until the present day. No one knew about it, not even her boyfriend.

Ms B felt she had some limited control over her bulimia. She was capable at times of eating normally, and her bulimia was mainly confined to when she was at home. However recently the bulimic urges had become more intense and Ms B feared that they would take over her life and she would no longer be able to keep this part of herself hidden.

This radical split between her external and her inner secret life also showed itself in how she thought about herself, what kind of a person she thought she was. To all outward appearances Ms B was a pleasant and likeable person, able to get on well with other people. At work she was well liked by her colleagues and pupils. But for Ms B the face she presented to the world was a false one. Behind it she felt herself to be an angry and nasty person, full of grievances against other people. For example she had been very close to her mother in her childhood and adolescence, and they still got on well together, although the relationship had now become more distant. However

Ms B actually thought her mother to be a self-centred person, incapable of really loving anybody, and she thought her mother had only been close to her because she had been lonely and needed companionship. Ms B had more affection for her father, but could not forgive him, because he had always seemed to prefer her older sister. She had many grievances against her boy-friend, all along the lines that he always put himself first and was only with her because he was desperate to get married and have children. All of these feelings were kept hidden, indeed Ms B felt sure that the people concerned had no inkling of how she really felt about them.

Ms B considered that her resentments against other people were justified, but at the same time she also judged herself to be an ungrateful and horrible person for having such hateful feelings towards others. She felt such feelings poisoned the relationships she had with the people she was close to, as they destroyed her love for them and, furthermore, led her to despise them for being taken in by her false front.

The only peace of mind Ms B could find was in her bulimia. In fact, although she was well aware of how pointless and self-destructive her eating disorder was, in a strange way she also felt that when she fully engaged in her bulimic ritual, she was being the most true to herself.

The bulimic urge was brought on by an intolerable feeling of emptiness which had to be filled. Ms B would then stuff herself full of food until she felt bloated. It didn't matter what food she thrust into her, in fact the more disgusting the combination and amount of food the more satisfaction she obtained. Once full to bursting, the initial sensation was one of content-ment and completion, the feeling of emptiness now entirely banished. She felt at peace with her body, which was no longer subject to the vicissitudes of needs or desires, and free from any demands from other people. However this contented state soon passed, and gradually changed into an unpleas-ant sensation of being bloated and overfull, that she was full of disgusting substances which she had to get rid of. Then Ms B would make herself sick by sticking two fingers down her throat and continued throwing up until there was nothing left in her stomach. This gave Ms B a wonderful sense of well-being. She felt purged of all the badness inside herself and cleansed of its noxious influence.

Although she found comfort in her bulimia, and could not see how she would be able to give it up, at the same time Ms B felt she could not go on like this and was desperate to gain control over her eating disorder. She asked the counsellor to support her in a determined effort on her part to lessen her dependence on bulimia, and the counsellor, seeing how self-destructive her eating disorder was, went along with this idea and offered her encouragement in trying to eat more normally. Initially Ms B reported that, with the counsellor's support, she felt less need for her bulimic rituals and was more able to eat nutritious food without vomiting it out. However after several sessions Ms B confessed to the counsellor that she had not been able to sustain this progress and that she had in fact returned to her previous pattern of bulimic eating, but had felt too ashamed to tell the counsellor.

The counsellor realized that going along with the idea that her role was to support Ms B in giving up her bulimia was in fact, merely reinforcing her already existing split between her public and secret life. In other words she had become enlisted into taking sides in Ms B's conflict (to stay bulimic or give it up) rather than helping her understand its meaning (see Chapter 2). Ms B's difficulty in giving it up was a sign that bulimia served some important purposes for her, and these needed to be understood before Ms B had any real chance of gaining some control over her eating behaviour. When the counsellor said to Ms B that she was not yet ready to think of giving up her bulimia, and that their first task was to understand it, Ms B was at first relieved that she would no longer have to pretend to the counsellor that she was mastering her eating behaviour. She took comfort from this demonstration that the counsellor would still value her and would carry on working with her, even if she was not actively trying to stop her bulimic behaviour. But she was reluctant to see that her bulimia had any meaning beyond what seemed to her to be its obvious purposes, namely to help her cope with the stresses in her life, to give her some relief from her feelings of emptiness and loneliness, and also to keep herself slim and attractive for her boyfriend.

The counsellor used the idea of an inner world of object-relationships to find a language with which to speak to Ms B about the possible meaning of her bulimia. The counsellor used a way of speaking which drew on Ms B's own words. For example, Ms B had described herself when bloated, as full of nasty things inside her. The counsellor elaborated such ideas and phrases of Ms B's into a meaningful pattern, through her use of the framework of an internal world. The counsellor put forward the idea, that her bulimia was a way of both dramatizing and also controlling a vicious internal fight between her good and bad objects. Ms B's constant anxiety was that her bad objects would destroy her good ones. Consequently Ms B used her eating behaviour as a desperate attempt to feed those good internal objects, which she felt to be weak and undernourished. However, her attempt to put goodness into herself failed, as she felt her greed and nastiness turned this goodness into something disgusting, which then had to be expelled.

This way of speaking conveyed to Ms B that her bulimic experience and behaviour was both meaningful and purposeful, a part of herself rather than something alien which had taken hold of her. As she came to accept this, she was able to take her part in this therapeutic conversation, so that the language used to make sense of her bulimia became truly a shared one. For example, she said on one occasion that it had occurred to her that the type of food she sometimes stuffed into herself, a disgusting mixture of sweet and sugary food, reminded her of the food her mother was most fond of. This led her to wonder whether what she was doing in her bulimia was taking in parts of her mother, in the hope that her mother could nourish her. However what then happened was that because these good aspects of her mother were taken in with greed and hatred, they were changed into bad ones, and then had to be expelled as quickly as possible before they took her over.

The idea of her bulimia as the enactment of an internal drama became most vivid and compelling when the counselling reached its most critical stage near the end, when the counsellor took on the aspect of one of Ms B's internal objects. Ms B clearly found the counsellor understanding and supportive, and told her so. But what remained hidden for some time was that she also experienced the counsellor, especially through her interpretations, as intrusive and controlling (just like Ms B experienced her mother). This led Ms B to become distant towards the counsellor, and in fact to break off the counselling for several sessions. When she returned, the counsellor was able to show Ms B how her internal drama of turning good into bad, of taking in and vomiting out, was now being enacted in the counselling itself. Ms B could now see her internal drama played out in front of her very eyes, and so more directly grasp how she used it to control the counselling (see Chapters 5 and 6 on transference).

By the end of the counselling Ms B was able to acknowledge for the first time that her bulimia was something she did to herself, rather than being something foreign, and that it had a purpose for her. This was the crucial first step in being able to gain some control over it. She felt strengthened and motivated to join a self-help group for people with eating disorders, something she would never have considered doing before she came to counselling.

Mourning and the depressive position

The concept of an internal world of objects in relationship with each other also throws more light on the experience of mourning, and in particular why it is such a painful and disturbing process, as in the case of Mrs A. Melanie Klein argued that a bereavement involves not only the loss of a person in the external world, but the threatened loss of one's inner objects as well.

> The poignancy of the actual loss of a loved person is, in my view, greatly increased by the mourner's unconscious phantasies of having lost his *internal* 'good' objects as well. He thus feels that

his 'internal' bad objects predominate and his inner world is in danger of disruption. We know that the loss of a loved person leads to an impulse in the mourner to reinstate the lost loved object in the ego. In my view, however, he not only takes into himself (reincorporates) the person whom he has just lost, but also reinstates his internalized good objects (ultimately his loved parents), who became part of his inner world from the earliest stages of his development onwards. These too are felt to have gone under, to be destroyed, whenever the loss of a loved person is experienced. (Klein, 1940, p. 156)

Faced with the loss of her internal good objects, which are derived from the loved parents, a series of anxieties are aroused in the mourner to do with guilt about having damaged the loving parents and sadness over their loss. If these anxieties can be tolerated, then the process of mourning can leave the mourner with more confidence in the robustness and goodness of their internal objects.

It seems that every advance in the process of mourning results in a deepening in the individual's relation to his inner objects, in the happiness of regaining them after they were felt to be lost ('Paradise Lost and Regained'), in an increased trust in them and love for them because they proved to be good and helpful after all. This is similar to the way in which the young child step by step builds up his relations to external objects, for he gains trust not only from pleasant experiences, but also from the ways in which he overcomes frustrations and unpleasant experiences, nevertheless retaining his good objects (externally and internally). (Klein, 1940, p. 164)

Klein called the constellation of anxieties and defences around loss and grief the *depressive position*. She characterized the depressive position as a nodal point of development, first established in infancy and reactivated every time the person is faced with similar states of mind as in mourning.

In developmental terms Klein described the depressive position as a state of mind in which the baby experiences depressive feelings which reach a climax just before, during and after weaning. It is melancholia in *statu nascendi*.

The object which is being mourned is the mother's breast and all that the breast and the milk have come to stand for in the infant's mind: namely, love, goodness and security. All these are felt by the baby to be lost, and lost as a result of his own uncontrollable greedy and destructive phantasies and impulses against his mother's breasts. (Klein, 1940, p. 148)

Klein hypothesized that, when hungry, the baby hallucinates or conjures up in its mind a breast full of milk. But if for whatever reason the breast does not appear or the baby cannot feed, then the image of an angry or withholding breast will be created. At this stage the baby will scarcely be able to imagine the mother as a separate person, but instead will omnipotently imagine the state of her body to be a product of his own feelings and impulses. He will therefore believe the breast has become angry or withholding as a response to his own hatred, aggression or greed.

In the depressive position the predominant mood is one of pining for the lost loved object (mother's breast and all it represents) and sorrow over the loss. Pining for the lost object implies dependence on it, and this can become an incentive to preserve and repair it. But dependence on others can also be feared, as it will bring about the same experience of loss and disillusion. The leading anxiety is that hatred will overcome love, that one's loved object will be damaged by one's anger and hatred occasioned by the experience of separation and loss. The main defences against such depressive anxieties are *manic* in nature. Feelings of loss or guilt can be denied through a sense of triumph or control over the loved object. Or an attitude of manic reparation can be adopted, for example, expressed in an over-protective and sentimental attitude towards the love-object, which is based on a fear of one's own aggression and of retaliation by the loved object rather than genuine concern.

These depressive feelings, anxieties and defences can be seen in the case of Mrs A. She described a constant state of restless anguish, a sense that she had lost something that could not be found. She found the experience of sadness or loss almost unbearable, and defended herself against these feelings by immersing herself in manic activity, flitting from one thing to another. She felt guilty towards others, for example her husband, for not loving or appreciating them enough. With her husband she kept such feelings at bay by needing to keep in constant contact with him, as though having to reassure herself that he was not damaged or destroyed by her 'bad' feelings towards him. She feared dependence on others, including the counsellor, as then she risked becoming prey again to the same feelings of loss and grief that are part and parcel of any attachment.

The depressive and paranoid-schizoid
modes of experience

*As well as these depressive experiences, Mrs A was also subject to feelings,
together with anxieties and defences, of a different order. When she felt at
her most fragile and desperate, she had a sense of dread. Both time and space
became constricted and threatening for her. Instead of an open future Mrs A
had the feeling that something terrible was about to happen. She developed
a fear of crowded places, in which space could no longer be trusted to keep
people at a safe distance from her, but threatened to implode (her agoraphobia was the other side of the claustrophobia revealed in her dream of being
entombed in her mother's coffin). Meaning and pleasure were sucked out
of her experience, leaving her feeling that life was pointless. Mrs A also
lost her sense of agency, feeling at the mercy of states of mind, such as her
bursts of uncontrollable crying or intrusive thoughts over which she had no
control.*

Klein called the constellation of such feelings and anxieties the
paranoid-schizoid position, which she envisaged as a counterpart to
the depressive position. In the paranoid-schizoid position it is the
very existence of the person and the world which is at stake, as persecutory and paranoid anxieties dominate. The leading anxiety
is that one's hatred of the loved object, occasioned for instance by
inevitable frustration around feeding at the breast, will result in
retaliation and persecution by this loved object, which will have
been transformed into a hating object. The intensity of the persecution experienced is such that the infant feels in danger of being
annihilated.

The main defences employed against this persecutory anxiety
are both more primitive and powerful than those of the depressive
position, and involve the splitting and/or evacuation of experience.
Experiences are *split* into good and bad, with a rigid distinction
between them so that the bad cannot contaminate the good and all
the good will be lost. Another way of controlling the bad is to *evacuate* it into the world outside, where it is felt to take over and control
people, leaving all the goodness inside oneself (this defence was
called projective identification by Klein).

Ms B is an example of someone whose predominant states of
mind and defences were of a paranoid-schizoid nature. Her bulimia
enacted a constant drama of the good becoming contaminated by
the bad and of the need to evacuate the bad in order to remain good.
By projecting the bad parts of herself into other people, she then

had the phantasy that she had turned them into nasty and selfish people. Such massive projection led her to feel constantly confused about the boundaries between herself and other people.

Klein saw the depressive and paranoid-schizoid positions as both developmental and structural concepts. She envisaged the infant initially passing through the paranoid-schizoid position, around the first few months of life, and then, if all went well, moving towards the depressive position. However she was careful to call these constellations of anxieties and defences 'positions' rather than stages, as she wanted to emphasize that they remain as permanent patterns in the mind throughout one's life. Each position can be seen as a 'mode of generating experience' (Ogden, 1992), and psychological change – whether in the course of a particular session or over a period of the counselling itself – can then be thought of in terms of shifts between these modes.

We can characterize the major distinguishing features of these two modes of experience as follows. Experience in a depressive mode involves the capacity to symbolize experience. Symbols, which achieve their most sophisticated expression in speech, are experienced as different from what they symbolize, and are thus able to represent what is experienced in a way that allows one to think about it. It is easiest to see what this means by seeing what happens when there is a failure to symbolize experience. In a classic paper on symbol formation the psychoanalyst Hanna Segal gave the example of a schizophrenic man who, on being asked why it was since his illness that he had stopped playing the violin, replied with some violence 'Why? Do you expect me to masturbate in public?' (Segal, 1988, p. 160). Segal called this *symbolic equation,* that is, there was no capacity to make a distinction between the activity, playing the violin, and what it might mean or represent in phantasy. There was no space for thinking in terms of 'as if' or 'being like'. So, for this patient, playing the violin was equivalent to or the same as touching his genitals in public.

For such a person, who cannot sublimate or symbolize his impulses and phantasies but feels controlled by them, there is no sense of agency. In the depressive mode, by contrast, one is able to take responsibility for one's actions. The achievement of symbol formation allows one to experience oneself as a person thinking one's own thoughts and feeling one's own feelings.

In the depressive mode of experience, projection (attributing parts of oneself to another) is used not only, or not primarily, as a way of evacuating parts of oneself into other people, as in the paranoid-schizoid mode, but also as a way of identifying with and understanding other people. Self and other are experienced as autonomous and separate. Other people (both in the external world and as internal objects) are experienced as 'whole objects', as people in their own right, rather than as 'part objects', that is primarily in terms of their body parts (e.g. breast) and function (e.g. feeding). The internal world becomes integrated to a sufficient degree to give continuity and stability to experience. Both self and other people are experienced as existing as more or less stable and unchanging over time, able to survive powerful changes in mood or feeling on one's part.

New experiences can be added to old ones without undoing or negating what has gone before. Historicity is created as the individual relinquishes reliance on omnipotent defences. The past is experienced as immutable, which brings sadness and resignation that one's past will never be all that one had wished.

As others are experienced as people in their own right, it becomes possible to care for them and feel concerned for them, as opposed to simply valuing them, as one would value a prized object or such essential objects as food or air. In the paranoid-schizoid mode other people are felt to be like things or substances in the world which can be damaged or used up. In the depressive mode other people can be hurt. Consequently one becomes capable of guilt, 'a specific sort of pain which one bears *over time* in response to real or imagined harm that one has done to someone about whom one cares. One can attempt to make reparation for that about which one feels guilty, but this does not undo what one has done' (Ogden, 1992, pp. 13–14).

In the depressive mode sadness, the experience of missing someone, loneliness and the capacity for mourning become dimensions of human experience. Because loss can be tolerated, the individual feels safe enough to make attachments to others and become intimate.

Experience in a paranoid-schizoid mode is dominated by the use of splitting or dissociation as a defence and a way of organizing experience. *Splitting* is based on the principle that one secures safety by separating the endangered from the endangering. Splitting is designed to manage the principle psychological dilemma in the paranoid-schizoid position, that the experience of loving and hating the same object generates intolerable anxiety. Ambivalence is too confusing and painful to face in this mode, as it tends to be equated with contamination. The problem is handled by forcefully separating loving and hating facets of oneself, as well as loving and hating facets of the object. Different aspects of self and object must also be kept rigidly separate from each other. Only in this way can the individual safely love the object in a state of uncontaminated security, and safely hate without the fear of damaging the loved-object.

Splitting in the paranoid-schizoid mode of experience is a much more radical form of defence than repression, which is more characteristic of depressive functioning. In repression the subject is in a kind of ignorance, knowing and not knowing about what is repressed at the same time. But in splitting we must imagine a fragmentation of experience so radical that it no longer coheres over time and space. The stability and continuity of experience can no longer be taken for granted, which makes knowing and thinking far more problematic. Instead there is the experience of magical or instant revelation.

> Each time a good object is disappointing, it is no longer experienced as a good object – nor even as a *disappointing* good object – but as the discovery of a bad object in what had been masquerading as a good one. Instead of the experience of ambivalence, there is the experience of unmasking the truth. This results in a continual rewriting of history such that the present experience of the object is projected backward and forward in time creating an eternal present that has only a superficial resemblance to time as experienced in the depressive mode. (Ogden, 1992, p. 19)

Splitting is an example of *omnipotent thinking* in which the complexities of loving and hating are magically resolved through the phantasy of controlling one's objects. Another example of omnipotent thinking is projective identification, the phantasy of forcing unwanted or bad parts of oneself into another person in order to damage and control him. Omnipotent thinking involves a denial of the separate existence of others. Instead other people are experienced primarily as consisting of projected and disowned parts of oneself.

The powerful need to separate the bad from the good creates a limited and dualistic range of experiences, with little room for subtlety or fine discrimination. The psychoanalyst Harold Searles quotes a patient

> I don't feel sadness; sadness isn't really something I feel ... I understand devastation and I understand rage and I understand terror; but I don't know the milder forms (she had referred to sadness as being a milder form of devastation) ... When I feel irritated or

annoyed, I don't really feel those feelings; what I feel is rage ... I can either feel complete devastation or nothing. I don't have those in-between states; they just never had a chance to develop. The others were too strong. So it's either those strong states or nothing, and most of the time it's been nothing .... (Searles, 1994, p. 294)

The continual rewriting of history together with the confusion between self and other leads to a brittleness and instability in object relations. There is an almost continuous backdrop of anxiety that things can never be trusted to be as they appear. A typical way of thinking in this mode, for instance, in relation to the counsellor, would be something like this: 'The fact of the matter is that I've deluded myself about you for a long time. It is obvious to me now that you have absolutely no regard for me, otherwise you wouldn't forget fundamental things about me like my girlfriend's name that I've mentioned a thousand times' (Ogden, 1992, p. 20).

In this mode of experience there is very little sense of subjectivity. Instead the self is primarily experienced as an object, as buffeted by thoughts, feelings, perceptions and impulses, as if they were external objects or forces occupying the self.

The value for the counsellor of thinking in terms of these two modes of experience is that it gives him a way of discriminating between clients in terms of their predominant mode of experience. For example, at first sight Mrs A and Ms B might seem to suffer from the same kind of difficulties, in that they are both preoccupied with loss. However, on closer scrutiny the quality of experience in each case is very different. For whereas Mrs A's problems were to do with the pain of loss, the death of her loved mother, Ms B never allowed herself to actually have the experience of loss or sadness. Indeed her bulimia seemed designed to protect her from having such feelings. She plunged from emptiness to satiation and then back to emptiness again. We can then see that a feature of Ms B's state of mind was, in fact, an *absence* of depression, an incapacity to mourn. It follows from this that, strange as it might sound, if Ms B were to make any progress, then she would need to be able to become depressed, to mourn what she had lost.

Once the counsellor has understood the client's predominant mode of experience, he can shape his interventions accordingly. For example, it would be more effective with a client whose experience is predominantly in the paranoid-schizoid mode to find a way of speaking to her which will resonate with her actual experience. As we have seen, because of the pull towards symbolic equation in this mode of generating experience, things are experienced concretely, with little sense of 'as if':

> One does not talk about the patient's feeling that he is like a robot, one talks with the patient about what it feels like to be a robot; one does not talk with the patient about his feeling that he is infatuated with a woman, one talks with him about what he feels when he believes he is possessed or haunted by a woman; one does not talk about the patient's wish to be understood by the therapist, one talks about the patient's conviction that the therapist – if he is to be of any value at all to the patient – must think the patient's thoughts and feel the patient's feelings. (Ogden, 1992, p. 22)

The depressive/paranoid-schizoid distinction also gives the counsellor a template for thinking about how a client's state of mind, as well as her anxieties and defences, can shift within a session, or over a series of sessions. With Mrs A, for instance, her more usual depressive position defences would collapse into more paranoid-schizoid ones, such as agoraphobia, at times of breaks in the counselling. The counsellor can also view the whole period of the counselling itself in terms of the client's capacity to become more capable of experiences in the depressive mode. So with Ms B one of the achievements of the counselling was that others came to be seen less as a receptacle of her disowned feelings, and more as people in their own right and for whom she could feel compassion.

(The paranoid-schizoid mode of experience will be further explored in Chapter 8.)

The Oedipus complex and the depressive position

In describing the Oedipus complex and the depressive/paranoid-schizoid modes of experience separately, the question arises as to how these two conceptual frameworks articulate with each other. In order to negotiate the various stages of the Oedipus complex, the individual would need to have developed sufficiently so that other people are not seen simply as extensions of oneself but as existing in their own right, and also capable of making relationships with others from which one might be excluded. Now this is one of the defining features of the depressive position. In other words, the capacity to negotiate the Oedipus complex, and the capacity to have experiences in the depressive mode are ways of describing a similar psychological and emotional constellation from different perspectives.

The paranoid-schizoid position is more linked to difficulties prior to negotiating the Oedipus complex. Indeed where paranoid-schizoid experiences dominate the picture an Oedipal structure may seem to be entirely lacking, as in the case of Ms B. The content of her sessions was about her relationship to her own body, or, later on in the counselling, about her relationship to the counsellor. Other people barely figured. When Ms B did talk about the people in her life with whom she was involved, such as her boyfriend or mother, they were described not as separate people, capable of making relationships with other people, but primarily in terms of their function in Ms B's life, just as she could only see other people relating to her out of their own need rather than out of any interest in or concern for her.

On closer examination, however, Oedipal themes in Ms B's material can be seen as hidden rather than absent (O'Shaughnessy, 1989). The apparent lack of an Oedipal dimension can be understood as a sign of Ms B's wish to exclude it from the relationship with the counsellor, and use the counselling to recreate a two-person, pre-Oedipal relationship. In the course of the counselling Ms B's fear and hatred of her sexual body, and her attempt through her bulimia to turn her body into a pre-sexual one became clear. She wished to create a kind of fused relationship with the counsellor, as though the world of other people did not exist.

It seemed that Ms B found the Oedipal scenario so frightening or disturbing that she retreated from it into a denial of its existence. This position has been called one of Oedipal illusion (Britton, 1989), the prime motive of which is to wipe out any sense of the parental relationship from which one is excluded. Although Ms B hardly ever talked about her parents as a couple – she preferred to see them only in relation to her, not to each other – the counsellor was left with the powerful impression that Ms B saw any coupling as potentially dangerous and destructive. With her boyfriend, for instance, although she could not bear the thought of losing him, she also dreaded intimacy with him as she then felt both invaded and controlled. She felt either totally immersed in the relationship with her boyfriend or utterly cut off from it. Either way she was unable to gain a perspective and so see her part in it.

Ronald Britton (1989) takes the ability of the individual to become an observer as well as a participant in a relationship as a crucial marker of both depressive position and Oedipal development. He argues that the establishment of a coherent and viable internal world, a mark of attaining the depressive position, is dependent on the successful negotiation of the Oedipus complex. Britton puts his emphasis not so much on the child's ability to tolerate the ambivalence of feelings with regard to each parent (which was Freud's emphasis), but on the child's ability to tolerate being excluded by the parental relationship. If, when confronted with this link between the parents, the child can manage the exclusion, and not be overwhelmed with jealousy or hatred and led to deny the reality of this link, then the child's internal world is felt to have a containing membrane. 'The closure of the oedipal triangle by the recognition of the link joining the parents provides a limiting boundary for the internal world. It creates what I call a "triangular space" – i.e. a space bounded by the three persons of the oedipal situation and all their potential relationships' (Britton, 1989, p. 86). Such a space includes the possibility of being an observer as well as a participant in a relationship, that is, the development in the child's mind of there being a third position, a witness of the parental relationship from which he is excluded. Once the possibility of observation is allowed then the child can also envisage being observed. The child is then able to see himself in interaction with others and entertain another point of view (that of himself being observed by another) while still retaining his own perspective, in other words a capacity 'for reflecting on ourselves whilst being ourselves' (Britton, 1989, p. 87).

The early stages of the Oedipus complex and gender identity

The depressive/paranoid-schizoid position schema can help in understanding the early stages of the Oedipus complex and the development of gender identity. In the case of Mrs A, for instance, she remembered resenting her mother as an adolescent, but never being able to understand why. In the counselling she came to understand this to be because her mother never conveyed a sense to her of being attractive to men.

Ogden throws some more light on how the relationship with one's parents crucially affects one's sense of gender identity by looking at the role of the mother in the early stages of the Oedipus complex. Freud came to realize that for the little girl, entry into the Oedipus complex involved a change of love-object, from the mother to the father. Ogden adds that this is not simply a change of object, but also a change in the quality of object. The pre-Oedipal mother, that is the mother to whom the child relates before the feelings associated with the Oedipus complex come into the picture, is more of an internal object, that is an object not completely separate from the child. But by the time the child is caught up in the Oedipus complex, the Oedipal mother has become an external object, like the Oedipal father, that is, an object which exists outside of the child's omnipotence. This is most clearly signalled by the fact that the Oedipal parents have a relationship with each other from which the child is excluded.

The pre-Oedipal mother, claims Ogden, has the task of mediating the little girl's entry into the Oedipus complex. He argues that the discovery of the Oedipal mother's externality is experienced as a betrayal.

> The child says, in effect, 'I thought we had an agreement that what's yours is mine and what's mine is yours, so why do I have to knock on the door of your bedroom (that you share with father) before going in? I didn't have to before'. The anger connected with this is directed more at the mother than at the father, since, in the little girl's mind, it is the mother who is 'defecting', 'changing the rules'. (Ogden, 1992, p. 119)

According to Ogden the mother mediates this transition by, symbolically letting the father into the relationship between herself and her daughter, while still retaining some of the closeness of the original, pre-Oedipal closeness. She does this by bringing in another perspective, that of the father, into her relationship with her daughter.

> The role of the mother as Oedipal transitional object is to allow herself to be loved as a man (her own unconscious identification with her own father). In so doing, she unconsciously says to her daughter, 'If I were a man, I would be in love with you, find you beautiful, and would very much want to marry you'. Since the unconscious mind knows nothing of 'If I were...', the mother's unconscious communication is more accurately stated as, 'I am a man, your father, and am in love with you, find you beautiful, and want to marry you'. (Ogden, 1992, p. 120)

In order to allow this to happen the mother allows herself to become what Ogden describes as the 'mother-as-father', that is an object that is creatively ambiguous in that it can embody aspects of both sexes and effect a transition between the two (this kind of object is based on what Winnicott [1951] called a transitional object). Before the little girl is capable of an Oedipal relationship with her father, experienced as an external object and subject to the intensity of her Oedipal feelings, she and her mother engage in a 'dress rehearsal', in which the girl can experience some of the quality of her potential Oedipal love for her father, but in the relative safety of her pre-Oedipal closeness with her mother. Ogden notes that this dress rehearsal is re-enacted in latency and adolescence in the 'shopping expedition', in which the daughter tries on clothes in front of her mother. Although the girl's father is physically absent in this scenario he is emotionally present, as it is 'to a large extent the father that the little girl sees in the mother's gaze' (Ogden, 1992, p. 120).

It is interesting from this perspective to reflect on Mrs A's relationship with her mother. She recounted instances of going shopping with her mother as a sign of their closeness when she was a teenager, but what she remembered was that they spent more time buying clothes for her mother rather than for her. Somehow, then, the normal Oedipal relationship between mother and daughter for Mrs A had become inverted: she was the one giving confirmation to her mother of her attractiveness rather than the other way round.

The little boy also has to deal with the change in the quality of the mother as object when he arrives at the threshold of the Oedipus complex. The task for him is to take as his love-object someone he experienced pre-Oedipally as omnipotent and only partly differentiated from himself. He is helped in this if he can experience masculine qualities in his mother with which he can identify.

By embodying aspects of both genders, each parent can help the child achieve a viable gender identity. In Ogden's view healthy gender development involves 'the creation of a dialectical interplay between masculine and feminine identities. This occurs when one does not have to choose between loving (and identifying with) one's mother and loving (and identifying with) one's father' (Ogden, 1992, p. 138). Successful negotiation of the Oedipus complex, and indeed of the depressive position does not therefore mean choosing one gender by repudiating the other. Such a repudiation would result in a pseudo-identity, designed to keep at bay the disastrous consequence of having to make an impossible choice. Ogden illustrates this in a dream of one of his patients, in which she was standing in the aisle of an airplane that was about to crash.

> The patient had to sit either with her mother on one side of the aisle or with her father on the other side. The patient knew that whoever she sat with would survive and that the other parent would die. The patient understood this dream as representing

a choice that she felt she had to make in which the outcome would be that half of herself would die. (Ogden, 1992, p. 138)

It follows from this account of gender development that the more the counsellor will help the client in their exploration of their gender identity the more he can embody aspects of both genders for the client.

Theory and belief

In this chapter I have described two of the most powerful psychoanalytic conceptual structures, the Oedipus complex and the depressive/paranoid-schizoid positions or modes of experience. Each provides an explanation for the client's distress or pain in terms of what went wrong with their development – failure to successfully negotiate the Oedipus complex, failure to achieve the depressive position – and consequently a goal for the counselling: a chance to have another go at what did not happen before. However neither model envisages an easy or even a wholly successful resolution. Although one can speak of a more or less successful or unsuccessful negotiation of the Oedipus complex, the feelings and conflicts associated with it never go away. Indeed, they are the stuff of life as all of us struggle to find ways of bringing love and desire together or of finding comfort from the pain of jealousy. Reaching the depressive position does not mean that paranoid-schizoid modes of experience have no value. If radical change is needed in one's life then the capacity to break links and fragment experience, marks of paranoid-schizoid functioning, will be necessary before new linkages can be made. The capacity for schizoid withdrawal and ruthlessness, both features of the paranoid-schizoid mode of experience, can be of great importance, for example, in matters requiring highly focused concentration and determination, where any matter which diverts attention away from the task in hand has to be kept firmly at bay.

Rather than simple models, then, with a clear structure and trajectory towards a definite outcome, the Oedipus complex and paranoid-schizoid/depressive position schema are better thought as grand or mythic narratives, each telling a complex and involved story about human development and the meaning of life. Freud and Klein themselves realized this connection between theory and narrative. Freud based the idea of the Oedipus complex on Sophocles' play *Oedipus Rex*. In her paper *On Identification* (1955), which gives one of her fullest accounts of the depressive and paranoid-schizoid positions,

Klein used a novel called *If I Were You* to illustrate her argument. The story is about a young man who is full of grievance about the misery of his life. He makes a pact with the devil to give up his soul in order to gain the power to enter the mind and body of other people and take them over (Klein felt here that the novelist displayed an intuitive understanding of the motive for and mechanism of projective identification). At first he uses this power selfishly, but he gradually discovers that he is able to feel concern for the people he inhabits. By the end of the story, as the devil comes to claim his soul, the young man dies more at peace with himself. Klein used this novel to illustrate how reaching the depressive position goes hand in hand with the development of a sense of moral awareness.

The student or trainee psychodynamic counsellor is faced with a problem regarding the use of theory. Inevitably he is put in the position of having to take on trust these conceptual and narrative structures, before he has had a chance to gain the clinical experience he needs in order to form a proper judgement as to their value or truth. The counsellor will only discover how useful these theoretical structures are by applying them, by seeing whether they make sense of the client's material in a session or over the course of the counselling. This sounds rather like asking the counsellor to believe in psychoanalytic theory as one might be asked to believe in a religious dogma.

A Jewish joke might throw some light on the nature of belief in this case.

A merchant visits his rabbi, a venerable and strictly observant sage, to complain about his son-in-law: 'He's a fanatic, he gets up at four in the morning, takes an ice-pick, goes to the river where he knocks a hole in the ice, and ritually immerses himself in the freezing water'. 'What's wrong with that?' asks the rabbi, 'You know I do the same'. To which the merchant replies, 'Yes, but he means it seriously'. (Aberbach, 1989, p. 93)

I take the merchant's reply not to imply that the rabbi does not value his beliefs and rituals – after all, as a rabbi he has based his whole life around his religion. But that is precisely the point. The rabbi has chosen this way of life, whereas it appears that what the merchant's son-in-law does is more of a compulsion. Furthermore the merchant implies that because the rabbi feels secure and at home in what he believes, he can afford not to take his beliefs too seriously, seeing them as just beliefs. Outside of the context of religious practice, the rituals in question are strange if not ridiculous.

So the counsellor can only come to believe in the theory when he has first-hand experience of it being able to generate meaning and understanding, for both him and his client in the consulting-room. And only when this confidence in the theory is sufficiently robust (normally after many years of practice) might he be able to discover the limitations of his theoretical perspective, as any point of view is bound to rule out other viewpoints. The more the experienced counsellor is able to find his own way of thinking and working, the more able he will be to judge the theoretical framework he has adopted, the series of grand narratives he has found persuasive, and see where they fail to do justice to his experience with his clients. At that point, I think, one could say that the counsellor, like the rabbi has reached a position where he can afford not to have to take his theoretical beliefs too seriously.

Summary

Psychoanalytic theory gives meaning to the client's experience and behaviour. It does this by providing a series of conceptual frameworks which function like maps, by means of which the counsellor can orient himself and find a sense of direction in the counselling.

Psychoanalytic thinking encompasses a developmental point of view, which views the client and her difficulties in terms of the developmental tasks and challenges appropriate to her stage of development. All of us need transitory symptoms and defences in order to cope with the normal anxieties and conflicts of living. However problems arise, and illness may result when these defences become rigid and powerful parts of the personality.

Psychoanalytic theory focuses on a dynamic understanding of states of mind by looking at the way anxiety and conflict are defended against by different parts of the mind, for example, through the mechanism of repression whereby unacceptable impulses and thoughts are pushed into the unconscious. What is repressed then finds expression in a disguised form, for example, as a symptom. The resistance of symptoms to change, as well as their strangeness and apparent meaninglessness, is because their roots lie in the unconscious.

Thoughts and feelings are experienced as unacceptable or unbearable when they appear to threaten the equilibrium of the mind. This may be the result of some particular external trauma. But there is also a nodal or critical point of development, called the Oedipus complex, which each individual has to negotiate and which is a potent and inevitable source of conflict and anxiety. The Oedipus complex is a constellation of relationships between the child and his or her parents. These form a template of how identification and the ambivalence of love and hate is managed by the child, and is crucial for the development of the capacity to observe and to think.

The figures of the Oedipus complex, the Oedipal parents and children, are based on the real family members but shaped by the individual's Oedipal fantasies, wishes and feelings. As such they function as internal objects, that is, as figures in the mind who stand in relationship to each other. Individuals can then be thought of as having an internal world peopled by objects, which are internalized versions of people in the external world, but now living a semi-independent existence in the mind. Understanding the kinds of objects in the internal world, and the relationships between them, can help the counsellor make sense of the quality and nature of the client's experiences and relationships with others.

Two different types of constellations of object-relationships, or modes of generating experience can be identified, the depressive and paranoid-schizoid. The depressive mode, or position as it was called by Klein, presupposes an ability to symbolize and integrate experience and to see oneself and others as whole persons. A whole range of feelings can be experienced, including those concerning loss and grief. In this mode ambivalence and conflict can be tolerated, which makes negotiation of the Oedipus complex a possibility. In the paranoid-schizoid mode, however, the consistency and continuity of experience cannot be taken for granted. Experience becomes fragmented, and persecutory anxieties dominate. Most people will oscillate between these two modes of generating experiences, although at any given period, or in any given counselling session, one mode will be more in evidence.

The Oedipus complex and depressive/paranoid-schizoid modes of experience can be thought of not only as conceptual systems but also as grand narratives, weaving the client's life experiences and history of relationships into a coherent story.

Further reading

Brown, D and Pedder, J (1979) *Introduction to Psychotherapy: an Outline of Psychodynamic Principles and Practice,* London: Tavistock.

Gomez, L (1977) *An Introduction to Object Relations,* London: Free Association Books.

Malan, D (1979) *Individual Psychotherapy and the Science of Psychodynamics*, London: Butterworths.

Segal, H (1964) *An Introduction to the Work of Melanie Klein*, London: Hogarth.

Swartz, S (2007) 'Oedipus Matters', *Psychodynamic Practice*, vol. 13, no. 4, pp. 361–74.

Waddell, M (1998) *Inside Lives: Psychoanalysis and the Growth of the Personality*, London: Duckworth.

5

TRANSFERENCE AND ITS MANIFESTATIONS

In the previous chapter we have looked at the meaning of the client's experience and behaviour through an investigation of the internal world and object-relations. There is one particular kind of object relationship to which both client and counsellor have immediate access, the relationship between client and counsellor. All forms of psychodynamic therapy are distinguished from other therapeutic approaches by their focus on the nature of this relationship, known as the transference. Turning one's attention directly onto the nature of the relationship between client and counsellor, focusing on what goes on in the room between the two, is an essential part of the psychodynamic approach, as we can see again in the case of Mrs A.

Mrs A: the nature of her transference onto the counsellor

Mrs A's attitude towards the counsellor started off in a mixed form. On the one hand she had a positive attitude towards counselling. She was motivated to seek help. She found that the counsellor's attention to the features of the setting enabled her to feel safe, and she found some of the counsellor's comments and interpretations helpful. This attitude was a sign of some ego-strength, that whatever difficulties she encountered in the course of the counselling, there was a part of her which could stand back as an observer and keep in mind the purpose of the counselling and its overall benefit for her.

Alongside this positive attitude was a more negative view. As it became clear, Mrs A found the counsellor himself cold and distant, too quiet and passive for her liking. These negative feelings towards the counsellor became apparent over her dislike of the way he ended the session. Once this could be talked about, and Mrs A discovered that voicing criticism of the counsellor did not bring about the disasters she feared – the collapse of the counselling, or retaliation by the counsellor – but, if anything, enabled her to have trust in the counsellor, she was then able to speak of some of her negative feelings towards him. She told him that, after their initial meeting, she had confided to a friend of hers that 'she liked the counselling but couldn't stand the counsellor'. She particularly disliked the way he always finished the session on time, even though she might not have finished telling him about something important. This demonstrated to her, she felt, that he was not interested in what she had to say, that he found her boring (see Chapter 2).

It later emerged that this was the same attitude she felt her father had towards her, and that being stopped by the counsellor at the end of each session reminded her of the way she had felt suddenly dropped by her father around the age of eight. At a still later stage of the counselling the attitude of coldness and indifference attributed to the counsellor seemed to resonate more with aspects of her mother, whose apparent attitude of warmth and love covered over a deeper lack of interest in her daughter's happiness and development. These links between her feelings towards the counsellor and those towards her parents made sense of her negative attitude towards the counsellor and thereby made her feelings more tolerable. At the same time seeing how these aspects of her relationships with father or mother had been 'transferred' onto the counsellor brought them to life in a particularly vivid and immediate way, and impressed upon her as to how she continued to treat other people as though she was still a rejected and hurt little girl.

These negative feelings towards the counsellor came and went throughout the counselling. They tended to die down after they were spoken about, but would reappear particularly around breaks in the schedule. They came to a head around the final long holiday break before the counselling was due to end. Mrs A returned from this break in a bleak mood. She said she now felt depressed again, and had restarted her antidepressant medication (which she had managed to give up shortly before the break). What was making her particularly depressed was that she had always relied on her husband's love and support, but over the holiday she had started to doubt that he actually loved her, and so she now felt distant towards him. At the same time, she was worried that her coldness towards him would anger him and make him want to leave her. Furthermore, she no longer had any faith in the counselling, she saw it all as pointless, and in fact she asked whether they could finish the counselling now rather than wait until the scheduled end in several weeks' time.

The counsellor could see that this serious turn in her marriage was a displacement of something that belonged to the counselling relationship. At this point instead of making her better, the treatment dominated by the prospect of ending, was making her worse. He could see that her doubt that her husband loved her, and her withdrawal from him, mirrored her probable feelings towards him (the counsellor), brought to a head by the break and the impending termination of the counselling. He therefore said to Mrs A that the return of her depression and her suspicious, cold and fearful feelings towards her husband were feelings that applied to the counsellor which were spilling over into her life outside the sessions. She felt abandoned by the counsellor both because of the break and because the counselling was coming to an end. As she still needed the counsellor's help, Mrs A felt it was too risky to acknowledge her feelings of rejection towards him, and so her husband had become a substitute target for her rage.

Mrs A's initial response was to protest that this was nothing to do with the counsellor, why did it always have to be about him. However, when the counsellor persisted and reminded her that in the sessions up to the break Mrs A had reported starting to feel better about herself which she had put down to the counselling, Mrs A was then thoughtful. After a long silence, during which Mrs A was much calmer, she then told the counsellor something which surprised him. She said that this was in fact not her first experience of counselling. About a year ago she had gone to see another counsellor, a woman, whom she had seen for several months, but had suddenly stopped going. It had always puzzled her why she had broken off the counselling, as she had liked the counsellor, who had been warm and supportive. She remembered in the last session she had attended she had started to complain about her husband not really loving her, not being as intelligent and sensitive as she was, and wondering whether he was really good enough for her. The counsellor had been sympathetic and encouraging. She had left the session feeling supported, but had then decided that, as she was feeling better, there was no point in continuing. She wrote a brief note to the counsellor thanking her for her help, but saying that as she now felt much better, she had decided not to continue.

Mrs A said she could now see that she had not really trusted this counsellor, who too easily took her side against her husband. The counsellor's attitude reminded her of her mother, who had never felt any of her boyfriends were good enough for her. The atmosphere in the counselling was warm and friendly, again rather like with her mother, which made it very difficult, as Mrs A could now see, for her to acknowledge that she might harbour negative or hostile feelings towards this counsellor.

In the rest of the session Mrs A was able to speak much more openly about feeling dropped by the counsellor and how she hated him for it. In subsequent sessions, coming up to the end of the counselling, she was able to link this to her rage with her mother for dying and leaving her feeling bereft. She now started to feel a much deeper sense of sadness about her mother's death and also a more genuine feeling of love towards her.

Freud and the discovery of transference

The example of Mrs A shows how the transference is a double-edged sword. On the one hand it poses the greatest danger to the counselling if the intensity of the client's feelings towards the counsellor get out of hand and are not contained within the counselling relationship. But on the other hand, if the transference relationship with the counsellor can be made safe enough for exploration, it can become the medium through which the client can experience in a powerful and vivid way those feelings, thoughts and object-relations which have been most violently repressed or split-off.

Freud was the first psychotherapist to systematically explore the nature of the transference. His writings display his own ambivalence about the transference, as to whether it posits a great danger to the therapy or whether it can be the therapist's greatest ally. His first therapeutic attempts with his patients relied on the idea of catharsis, that patients would get better if they were able to express their suppressed feelings and thoughts. To this end he employed hypnosis in order to get his patients to remember traumatic situations or events and then give voice to and work through the powerful affects produced (a process he called abreaction). However he increasingly found this procedure unreliable. For example, the most brilliant results might suddenly be wiped out if the patient no longer trusted him as the therapist. However, if he were able to restore this breach in the relationship with the patient, then the work would once more continue to be productive. But this personal relationship between patient and therapist was not something he initially knew how to address in the therapy. This can be seen in his account of an incident with a female patient, 'with whom hypnotism had enabled me to bring about the most marvellous results, and whom I was engaged in relieving of her suffering by tracing back her attacks of pain to their origins. As she woke up on one occasion, she threw her arms round my neck' (Freud, 1925, p. 27). This sudden eruption of the patient's sexual feelings towards Freud brought the hypnotic treatment to a sudden end. Freud thought that the patient's feelings were not really about him – 'I was modest enough not to attribute the event to my irresistible personal attraction.' Instead Freud saw that he had become the recipient of some powerful repressed feelings which had their origin elsewhere, for example in the Oedipal scenario. This phenomenon he called transference, a form of projection in which feelings, thoughts and experiences which belong to another person or situation are displaced onto the figure of the therapist and the relationship between therapist and patient.

There is a widely held belief that transference is a dangerous thing which, ideally should be kept out of the therapy, and, if it is to appear, needs to be kept strictly under control. One often hears the idea that therapy must not in any way encourage the patient to become dependent on the therapist, for fear the patient (and the therapist) will stay imprisoned in this dependency forever.

But not addressing the transference does not mean it will simply go away. The consequences of choosing to stay in ignorance of the transference are evident from the case of Mrs A. With her first counsellor the negative transference was never addressed and so became *acted out* in Mrs A's sudden termination of the counselling, that is the feelings and thoughts involved were discharged through behaviour rather than being subject to thought and understanding.

From initially seeing the transference as the most powerful form of resistance to the counselling, as the eruption of primitive impulses and feelings with the aim of disrupting any further progress in the therapy, Freud came to see the transference as having the potential to become the most potent part of the therapist's armoury. He saw transference as a form of *repetition*, in which the patient repeated with her therapist all of her old and established ways of relating to significant figures in the past.

> The decisive part of the work is achieved by creating in the patient's relationship to the doctor – in the 'transference' – new editions of the old conflicts; in these the patient would like to behave in the same way as he did in the past, while we, by summoning up every available mental force (in the patient), compel him to come to a fresh decision. Thus the transference becomes the battlefield on which all the mutually struggling forces should meet one another. (Freud, 1915, p. 454)

In directly addressing the transference with the client the counsellor is in effect appealing to the client's capacity to observe her own behaviour and think about it. So Mrs A was able to manage the transference onto the counsellor, of her ambivalent relationship with her mother, when the links between the two could be clearly perceived by her, as they were when she first felt safe enough to speak of her hostile feelings towards the counsellor. However she then lost this capacity for self-observation around the final break, with the counselling due to end shortly, when she found herself almost completely taken up with her feelings towards her counsellor. At this point, she later told the counsellor, her feelings about him were so intense that she felt she was going mad, which was the main reason why she went back to her GP to restart her antidepressant medication.

This narrowing of the client's attention onto the figure of the therapist, to the virtual exclusion of all other concerns, can be alarming to the client, as well as the counsellor. However, by the very fact that the transference now looms so large, its nature can more clearly be seen and therefore worked through.

Types of transference

We have seen with Mrs A that the transference can take different forms. There was first of all a *positive transference* established. This was evident from Mrs A's ability to engage in the counselling and trust the counsellor to understand her sufficiently in order to help her. These attributes were modelled on the 'good' qualities of her parents and other helpful figures in her life.

If a positive transference is not established it will be much harder for a *working alliance* (sometimes called the 'therapeutic alliance') to be set up between counsellor and client. This term is used to describe the way client and counsellor can work cooperatively together on the client's problems. The working alliance with the counsellor is what sustains the client through the inevitable pain and frustration which any kind of therapeutic treatment involves.

Mrs A was also at times hostile towards the counsellor, telling him she found him cold or harsh towards her. This was her *negative transference* towards him, and she was relieved when these critical feelings towards the counsellor were brought out into the open and their nature and roots explored. Indeed the very fact that her negative transference could be acknowledged played a large part in Mrs A being able to trust the counsellor, and so significantly strengthened her positive transference towards him. Sometimes the negative transference is evident, but often it lies hidden behind an attitude of either compliance or idealization on the client's part (this is illustrated in the next section).

In addition to the positive and negative transference, another type of transference made its appearance towards the end of Mrs A's counselling.

In one session, in a rather embarrassed if not coy way, Mrs A commented on the smart clothes the counsellor was wearing – she had never previously made any comment about the way the counsellor dressed; in fact had never really in any overt way treated him as though he was both human and gendered. In another session Mrs A herself came in smarter and brighter clothes, and made several teasing remarks to the counsellor about the way he conducted himself in the session. She wondered aloud whether he was married and what his wife might say about all the female clients he saw.

In Mrs A's rather flirtatious attitude towards him, the counsellor could see the emergence of an *erotic transference*. In this instance he chose not to draw Mrs A's attention to it, preferring to simply remark on how much better Mrs A was now feeling about herself. He did this because he saw in Mrs A's rather sexual behaviour towards him not only a repetition (most clearly of her relationship with her father before he withdrew from her) but also evidence of *something new* in the relationship with the counsellor. It was as though Mrs A was experimenting with being serious and playful at the same time, or bringing together affection and desire. To comment on it risked becoming heavy-handed and thus taking away from the spontaneity of Mrs A's behaviour with him.

In fact all types of transference have this ambiguity, of being a repetition of a past object-relationship, but a repetition that is never exact, and so leaving room for something that never happened before. Freud in fact described experiences in the transference as being 'of a provisional nature', occupying 'an intermediate region between illness and real life' (Freud, 1912, p. 154). This intermediate region between illness and life is also a way of describing the counselling setting, and we can see how the counselling setting creates the conditions not only for the counsellor's container function (see Chapter 2) but also for the development, elucidation and management of the transference.

Illustrations of the negative transference

The type of transference that many counsellors have most difficulty with is the negative transference, as this is the one that is most threatening to the image of counselling, of a kindly counsellor whose work with the client is rewarded by her admiration and gratitude. In fact the negative transference, in some form or other, will always be present in a counselling relationship, as the client is bound to enact with the counsellor her unsatisfactory or failed relationships which directly or indirectly brought her into counselling.

Often the negative transference only becomes evident in the way the client adapts to the setting. For example with Mrs A, her anger with the counsellor emerged over the issue of the ending of each session and the holiday breaks in the sequence. With Mrs A, a good enough working alliance had already been established before the negative transference came to be addressed. But with some clients the negative and hostile feelings towards the counsellor are so dominating that he may have little choice but to deal with them from the very beginning, and in fact the very viability of the counselling may depend on his being able to do so.

Mr C came to the Student Counselling Service of the university where he was studying because he was very depressed after having failed his exams. He was seen by a female counsellor, who offered him a contract of 16 sessions. Mr C was not able to think about why he had failed his exams, beyond blaming the examiners for incompetence. He was openly contemptuous of the counsellor, putting her immediately on the defensive by asking about her qualifications, and criticizing her for what he took to be her defensive body posture and the angry tone of her voice. He was dismissive of any attempt on her part to offer understanding or interpretation, either saying that what she said he knew already, or insisting that words were of no value to him, what he needed was action.

What did seem to offer a way forward for the counsellor was that from time to time this very arrogant and aggressive front would suddenly collapse, and Mr C would become desperate and pathetic. He would implore the counsellor to help him, saying he could no longer cope with his life. It was clear that failing his exams had been experienced by Mr C as a traumatic blow, shattering his self-image as a brilliant student. However, as soon as the counsellor started to show sympathy towards Mr C and his plight, he would retreat again into his arrogant denigration of the counsellor.

The counsellor came to see that the best way of getting anywhere with Mr C was to directly address his negative transference towards her, which was preventing Mr C from deriving any benefit from the counselling. Thinking in terms of transference helped her to take out the 'personal' element of Mr C's transference to her and see in his attitude, a powerful re-enactment of a primitive and disturbed object-relation.

She therefore drew Mr C's attention to his arrogant and contemptuous attitude with her, and told him she saw it as a defence against showing any vulnerability to her, which he dreaded. Mr C was momentarily stopped in his tracks by this remark, before dismissing it contemptuously as 'text-book therapy'. The counsellor, however, would not allow herself to be deterred.

Every time Mr C displayed his arrogant attitude towards her, she took up with him what it was he could not bear to recognize in himself, or bear her to see in him.

Mr C continued to dismiss the counsellor and her attempts at helping him, but towards the end of the counselling this attitude softened as he saw he had not destroyed the counsellor through his aggression. He was able to acknowledge his overwhelming dread of being vulnerable, which in his mind meant being totally at the mercy of someone bent on sadistically harming him (this was the object-relation being repeated in the transference). The counsellor's ability to tolerate this helped Mr C become less self-critical and devastated by not having passed the exams, and to take responsibility for his failure rather than blaming it on others.

Often the negative transference lies hidden behind what might seem at first sight to be a positive attitude on the part of the client, but which on closer examination turns out to be a façade, behind which is hidden the client's anger with or hostility towards the counsellor. This sometimes finds expression in the client's *idealization* of the counsellor, in which he is treated by the client as though he is beyond criticism and without flaw. The purpose of this idealization is to cover up the client's hostility to or disappointment with the counsellor. The difference between a positive and idealizing transference is that the positive transference becomes something on which the client can build upon in making changes in the work. But in the idealizing transference no real progress can be achieved in the work until the idealization is dismantled and the underlying negative feelings brought out into the open. The consequences of not addressing the client's idealization of the counsellor are illustrated in the following example.

Mr D, a young man with a very traumatic background, in which he had been physically abused by his mother and neglected by his father, was seen by a female counsellor in a GP practice. He came for counselling saying he could not cope with relationships, was desperately lonely and could see no future for himself. In view of his terrible background the counsellor was able to offer him more sessions than was normally possible, and made a contract with him for one year. In the counselling Mr D described a childhood of unremitting misery, in which he lived in terror of his mother's rages, which sometimes resulted in her beating him. His father had left when he was small, unable to put up with his wife's violence towards him as well as his son. This left Mr D feeling that his father had simply abandoned him to his mother's cruelty.

The counsellor felt under enormous pressure not to repeat any of this cruel and abandoning behaviour, in fact to try and give Mr D an experience of being cared for. Although she was at times aware of feeling irritated or critical of Mr D, for example he was often late for his sessions, she felt he was so fragile that he would not be able to cope with any indication of anger or displeasure on her part, as she would then be experienced as just like his mother. She addressed his lateness in terms of his not believing that anyone would be interested in him, an interpretation he agreed with, although this interpretation did not make any difference to his persistent lateness.

Mr D was openly appreciative of the help he was getting from the counsellor. He said he felt listened to and understood for the first time in his life, finding what the counsellor had to say both insightful and compassionate. Several times he talked about how totally different the counsellor was from his mother and from all the other women he had encountered in his life, who had all misused or betrayed him.

However despite this attitude of admiration and gratitude towards the counsellor his life outside did not improve. He continued to feel miserable and lonely outside the sessions. The counselling itself started to take on a predictable quality, in which Mr D would come and tell more stories about his cruel mother, cowardly father or exploitative girl-friends, and the counsellor would try to help him acknowledge his feelings, which he found hard to tolerate, and come to terms with what had happened in the past. In view of his failure to change, the counsellor tried even harder to show compassion for Mr D and his predicament, feeling that the impasse in the counselling was due to her inability to understand him sufficiently for him to feel safe.

After about six months, to the counsellor's surprise Mr D did not show up for the first session after a break. In fact he never came again, and did not reply to any of the counsellor's communications. The counsellor was left feeling hurt, confused and angry – in short, a failure.

It took the client's abrupt termination of the counselling for the counsellor to see how she had all too willingly gone along with Mr D's idealization of her. This had prevented her from seeing the negative transference hidden behind the idealization, which was never addressed, and was the reason why the counselling made no progress.

The material of the sessions, together with some of the counsellor's own feelings and reactions to the client, pointed to a more complex picture of Mr D than the one-dimensional image the counsellor had constructed of him as a helpless and passive victim of his mother's violence and his father's abandonment of him. This left out of the picture the ways in which Mr D also identified with these aspects of his parents. In other words, the counsellor saw only one side of the object-relationships in Mr D's internal world, in which a cruel object was paired with a submissive one, and an abandoning object with an abandoned one. Consequently the counsellor did not want to see how Mr D could also be capable of violence and cruelty and of abandoning anyone he got close to, as in fact he had shown by abandoning the counsellor in his abrupt termination of the counselling.

One might wonder why the counsellor colluded with this idealization of her? Maybe she felt flattered by Mr D's apparent admiration of her. It is likely she felt gratified by his apparent appreciation of her work, as the work itself, in which the counsellor invested an enormous amount of energy but which failed to help her client change, offered her no rewards. Another reason the counsellor might have played her part in establishing and maintaining the idealization is to do with what Mr D had projected into her. Mr D was very frightened of his own rage and potential for violence, which made him feel he was just like his mother, and this fear was projected into the counsellor, who acted as though it would be too frightening and too much for Mr D to bear if his underlying rage and hostility were brought to light (see the description of projective identification in Chapter 4).

By not addressing the negative transference, the counsellor deprived Mr D of an opportunity to test out, in the safe setting of the counselling, how realistic his fears of his potential for violence might be. This is what Mrs A was able to do, that is experience at first hand that her anger with and hatred of her counsellor did not actually destroy or damage him, as she feared it would. The irony in the case of Mr D is that by not addressing the negative transference, the counsellor brought about the very situation which she had striven so hard to avoid. She had tried to bolster Mr D's confidence and belief in himself by only focusing on what she saw as the positive features of his personality. But by treating Mr D with kid gloves, by responding to him as though he was too damaged or fragile to face his own rage and hatred as well as his disappointment in relationships, she was in fact confirming his worst fears about himself. That is, she was endorsing his view of himself as someone who really was pathetic, weak and cowardly – just as he felt he had been for his mother in submitting to her violence, and just like his father had been in Mr D's eyes by abandoning him to his mother.

Illustrations of the erotic transference

The erotic transference covers those feelings the client may have for the counsellor which are best described as falling in love. The client's love for the counsellor may have non-sexual elements, for example the sense of a deep and special friendship with the counsellor. But it is the sexual attraction or excitement which usually accompanies the client's erotic feelings, which is likely to make the erotic transference seem so difficult to address.

Just as with the idealizing transference, the erotic transference can serve a defensive function, for example, to hide the negative transference. But, as with all forms of transference, it can also be the expression of something provisional or new for the client, the emergence of a part of herself which she has hitherto kept hidden or denied. This double-sided nature of the erotic transference is illustrated in the following example.

Mr E was a lonely and depressed man in his late forties seeing a young female counsellor in a counselling agency. He had come for help with problems at work and for depression. The counsellor had offered him a contract of up to a year.

Mr E had had only one previous intimate relationship with a woman, who had left him for another man. He had a very close and stifling relationship with his mother, whom he felt he had to please, and a distant relationship with his father. He continued to live at home with his parents. He had no siblings, and spent his time at home on his computer, or going out in the company of a handful of male friends.

At first he was suspicious and haughty towards the counsellor. When this attitude was pointed out to him by the counsellor, he was able to say that he behaved in this way because he expected her disapproval and disdain. Once he was able to explore these feelings he became more involved in the counselling, and started to trust the counsellor with some of his more secret feelings. Very slowly and warily Mr E started to tell the counsellor of some of his sexual thoughts and fantasies about his female work colleagues, which evinced considerable embarrassment and awkwardness on his part.

As the counselling progressed Mr E started to say that he was feeling better. Indeed he looked better, and in fact was now dressing in better fitting and more expensive clothes than before. He started to display an interest in the counsellor's life outside the sessions, for example asking her before one of the breaks where she was going on holiday, who was she going with and so on. He gently chided her when she did not answer.

The counsellor was unsure whether to speak of this now evident erotic transference on Mr E's part. It did not seem to be a problem, in fact Mr E was positively blooming in the counselling. She feared that addressing the sexual nature of their relationship would be disturbing and confusing for Mr E. He might experience it either as a sign that the counsellor disapproved of his sexuality, which would have been a repetition of his relationship with his mother, who had never affirmed his attractiveness or potency as a man. Or he might feel the counsellor was trying to involve him in some sort of illicit sexual relationship, this time a repetition of his mother in a different guise, as an Oedipally alluring figure who was trying to entrap him.

The situation came to a head in the session before the first Christmas break, when Mr E came into the session carrying an expensively wrapped gift box, which he offered to the counsellor, saying, 'I've bought you a little gift to say thank you for all the good work you are doing with me.' He added that he would like the counsellor to open the present when she got home. It was tempting for the counsellor to simply accept the gift and get on with the session, but she knew that she needed time to try to reflect about its meaning and implications for the counselling. In order to give herself time to think she thanked Mr E for his present, and said she would put it down on the table next to her for the time being. Mr E was a bit surprised by her reaction, but he sat down and started the session.

As she gathered her thoughts together over the course of the session the counsellor realized she was caught in a dilemma. Her first thought was that she had no choice but to accept Mr E's present, for her to refuse it would be a crushing rejection. However she was an experienced enough counsellor to know that it is never advisable to act under a feeling of compulsion, as one is bound to be acting out some aspect of the transference. Once she allowed herself the thought that she did have a choice about saying no, she could then see that, in fact, she also felt very uncomfortable about accepting Mr E's gift. It was not so much whether she should accept any gift from Mr E – after all giving a gift at Christmas is part of everyday, polite behaviour – it was more about the expensiveness of the present and also the manner in which he was giving it, giving her no choice about accepting it and furthermore asking her to unwrap it when she got home. The counsellor realized she felt controlled by Mr E's actions, that she was being tacitly forced into a certain kind of relationship with him. This relationship was clearly an erotic one, and the counsellor now felt it was important that she did not accept the gift, as to do so would mean that she was colluding in and encouraging him in his erotic transference towards her. In effect, she concluded, by accepting his gift she would be stoking up his sexual feelings only to inevitably let him down every time she ended a session, went on holiday and, indeed, came to terminate the counselling. To accept his gift would then be tantamount to acting like his past girlfriend, who had gone out with him, only in the end to betray him, or like his mother, whom Mr E felt had rendered him unable to cope well with living in the world by making him too dependent on her.

The content of the session lent further weight to the counsellor's musings. There was a story of his need to placate a controlling female boss at work, who used her authority to belittle and humiliate him. Mr E also spoke of another female colleague at work whom he felt was leading him on by making flattering comments about him, but, he said, 'she's only doing this because she wants something from me, she wants me to help her with some new software for her computer'. The counsellor felt these stories of being controlled, humiliated and exploited by women were a commentary on how he might experience her, and that accepting his gift would only serve to distract from an exploration of this negative transference.

The counsellor waited for a suitable opportunity before the end of the session, and then said that she wanted them to think together about his present to her. She thanked Mr E again for his gift. She said she would like to accept his gift, and appreciated his gratitude for her help. However, she also thought his present expressed more than his gratitude towards her, that it also expressed his wish to have a relationship with her, for her to become his lover, and that was not possible. For her to accept his gift would therefore mean that she was leading him on, and promising a relationship with him which she could not give him.

Mr E was crestfallen by the counsellor's response. He said he was very hurt by her reaction and felt rejected. However, he admitted that he was now having sexual fantasies about her, which made him feel both embarrassed and frightened. It was a relief to be able to admit to these and bring them out into the open. He could see that it was not appropriate for the counsellor to accept his gift. He decided to take his gift back, and in fact, in discussion with the counsellor, he said there was a woman in his office whom he liked and that it would be a good idea to give the present to her. He left the session still feeling hurt and rejected, but also relieved.

Over the course of the counselling Mr E was able to speak more of his sexual feelings and fantasies concerning the counsellor and to no longer feel so ashamed or frightened of them. Her saying no to his gift reassured him that expressing sexual feelings to the counsellor did not mean they had to be acted upon, and that his sexuality could be accepted by the counsellor without endangering their relationship. He often spoke of her courage in saying no to him as a turning-point in the counselling. He realized he had never said no to his mother in her demand for an over-close relationship with him, nor had his father been able to stand up to her on his son's behalf. He also came to see that in bringing the counsellor a present he was trying to avoid the pain and sadness of the coming Christmas break, that he feared being separated from her. In saying no to his gift, the counsellor had implicitly conveyed to him that she believed he was strong enough to bear the separation from her.

Although he could acknowledge all this, Mr E also never really forgave the counsellor for refusing his gift. By saying 'no' to him the counsellor put him in touch with the negative feelings which lay hidden beneath his erotic transference. He was angry with the counsellor, indeed hated her for her power to humiliate and control him. Once both the erotic and the negative transference could be brought out into the open, and Mr E was able to see that the counsellor did not reject him because of his loving or his hostile feelings towards her, the positive transference became strengthened and Mr E became more confident and assertive both with the counsellor and with people in the world outside.

Sometimes, as with the negative transference, the counsellor can come across a more intense and overt form of the erotic transference, in which the whole relationship between client and counsellor takes on a sexualized form. In such cases it is important that the counsellor finds a way of managing this eroticized transference in order to preserve the counselling.

Ms F came for counselling at a counselling agency complaining of an inability to sleep and concentrate. She asked to see a female counsellor, but as none was available, started counselling with a male counsellor with a contract of one year. She soon revealed a long history of sexual abuse by her father. Shortly after this she started to speak of her fear that the counsellor was having sexual feelings about her, and this was making her have sexual thoughts about him. She said that between sessions she could not stop herself from thinking about making love to the counsellor, a thought which both excited and disgusted her.

Ms F became very frightened and disturbed by her sexual feelings towards the counsellor. In particular she could not work out whose sexual feelings these were, hers or the counsellor's, and this confusion was extremely distressing. Ms F felt the counselling was now making her worse, for example she had started up again a relationship with an ex-boyfriend who treated her in an abusive way.

There followed a period of sexualized tension, with Ms F finding herself compelled to speak of the circumstances of the sexual abuse with her father, her sexual activity with her ex-boyfriend, and her sexual feelings towards the counsellor. Speaking to the counsellor about her sexual life brought her some relief and understanding, but it also made her more and more excited, and at the same time more and more frightened of arousing the counsellor and hence precipitating a sexual relationship between them. It was clear that at times for Ms F there was scarcely any distinction in her mind between speaking to the counsellor about her sexual feelings about him and actually having sex with him.

For his part, the counsellor considered terminating the counselling and finding a female counsellor to carry on with Ms F. However he also thought that alongside the alarming nature of Ms F's eroticized transference, there was also a working alliance between them, albeit a rather fragile one. In other words, he felt there was a part of Ms F not caught up in the sexualization of the transference, and to which he could speak in order to make sense of what was happening in the sessions. To end the counselling at this point would then probably be more of a response to Ms F's fear of her own sexuality. Instead he resolved to try and continue working with Ms F and see if these fears could be addressed.

In view of Ms F's profound confusion around sexuality, and her tendency towards thinking in terms of symbolic equation (see Chapter 4, p. 78) the counsellor thought that speaking to Ms F about the sexual component of her feelings towards him would only confuse and frighten her more. She would be likely to experience such an attempt on his part as though he wanted to initiate some form of sexual activity between them, and so as a re-enactment of the sexual abuse. The counsellor decided to help Ms F think of her sexual arousal as a way of coping with her anxiety about intimacy. He took a clear and consistent line of interpreting her compulsion to speak about her sexual thoughts and feelings towards him as a way of defending herself against her wish to trust the counsellor and to be understood by him. This refusal on the counsellor's part to join in the state of sexual excitement and confusion functioned as a kind of Oedipal barrier in the room, reinstating the incest taboo. Over time, the sexual tension lessened sufficiently for Ms F to be able to think with the counsellor about the meaning and purpose of her compulsive sexual thoughts.

The social dimension of transference

We have seen how the client transfers her feelings, thoughts and object-relationships onto the figure of the counsellor. In fact transference can be thought of as the projection of what Melanie Klein called a 'total situation (see Joseph, 1989), the network of object-relationships which make up the client's inner world, formed out of the events and relationships of the client's early life. These states of mind are both personal to the client, but also part of her family constellation.

However the transference is not only individual and familial, it also has a wider dimension, as each client and counsellor has a social as well as a personal identity. The client's experience, the make-up of her object-relationships and inner world, is a product not only of her membership of her family, but also of a particular culture, ethnic group, social class, gender, sexual orientation and such other. The counsellor will need to keep in mind how these social transferences might impinge on the counselling relationship. He will need to listen carefully to the particular transference meaning each client will find in the perception and experience of social similarity and difference, as the following two vignettes illustrate.

A white, female counsellor working with a black, female client was alive to the possibility of persecution and misunderstanding on the part of her client, who had suffered from white prejudice. While this was in evidence in the transference, for example, the client treating the counsellor as though she had superior knowledge and status, the counsellor sometimes found the reverse situation played out, where the client treated the counsellor as inferior and an object of pity. When the counsellor brought this to the client's attention, it emerged that this represented an aspect of the client's relationship to her sister and her mother, both of whom were darker-skinned than the client. For the client's family, to be dark-skinned was a mark of inferiority. When, in discussion, the counsellor said, 'but I am white, and therefore lighter-skinned than you', the client replied, 'of course you are white, but you are actually very dark-skinned for a white person' (the counsellor was in fact of Mediterranean origin). It then became clear, to both counsellor and client, that the client took this feature to be a mark of racial or cultural inferiority on the counsellor's part, which was why she related to the counsellor as though she were to be pitied.

A male counsellor working with a male, homosexual client was able to help the client explore his fear of the counsellor's homophobia (the client took the counsellor to be heterosexual, although he made it clear that he would not expect a homosexual counsellor to be free of homophobia). Once the client felt more accepted by the counsellor, he was then able to explore his envy of the counsellor's heterosexuality, in the sense of as he put it, 'you are the man my mother would have hoped to have as her son'. At a later stage in the counselling, the counsellor (who was heterosexual), found himself admiring, if not envying the client's ability to love another man, a feature he recognized as repressed in his own make-up as a heterosexual male. This realization on the counsellor's part was an important counterweight to something that he did not want to acknowledge in himself that he had a wish that the client give up his homosexuality and become heterosexual. The counsellor felt ashamed to acknowledge this wish to himself, feeling it was not 'politically correct' to have such a thought, and that it was a product of his membership of a homophobic culture. However, once he was able to find value in the client's homosexuality, he could more readily see his wish to cure his client of his homosexuality as a projection from the client, representing that part of the client that wished he was heterosexual.

What these examples show is that it is essential with each client to take account of the impact of social, cultural and racial factors, as these 'social facts' are part of our experience in the world. But they also show that the meaning of these social facts cannot simply be taken for granted or known in advance, they have to be discovered in the course of the counselling.

(A summary and suggestions for further reading for this chapter will be found at the end of Chapter 6.)

6

Working in the Transference

How to recognize transference

We have seen in the previous chapter that sometimes the intensity and compelling nature of the transference becomes obvious, but more often it is experienced as something going on quietly, in the background of the session. How, then, can the counsellor recognize the transference when it is often not in direct view?

There are three main ways of recognizing transference. These are: by *observing* the way the client conducts herself in the session, by *listening* to the content and process of what she says, and by *registering* the impact of her behaviour and speech.

Observing the client means taking account of how the client looks, speaks and acts in the counselling sessions, and then trying to put a name to her demeanour so that it can be thought about. Observing the client means trying to discern patterns or regularities in the way the client conducts herself in the session. For instance over time Mrs A's counsellor recognized a pattern in the way she responded to his comments or interpretations, namely that she would typically dismiss what he said. This dismissive attitude on her part was also expressed by her body, as she would often turn slightly away from him whenever he started talking to her. These observations helped him think about the kind of object-relationship being played out in the transference, for instance whether Mrs A experienced him as intrusive or critical and therefore protected herself by ignoring what he said.

In listening to the content of the session the counsellor needs to bear in mind the context in which the client speaks, namely that whatever the client talks about is said in the presence of the counsellor, and so is in some way addressed to him. With this in mind, when listening to the client's stories of people and events in her life, the counsellor might also be able to discern some indication of the client's experience of him. So, for instance, in Mr E's stories of being controlled by his boss and led on by another colleague, the counsellor found helpful references to the kind of object-relationship being recreated in the transference.

Further evidence regarding the transference, in fact all of the client's object-relations, can be gleaned not only by what the client says but also by the way in which it is said. In other words the counsellor needs to listen to process as well as content. This might mean noting the regular patterns which emerge in the client's mood or feelings in a session or over a number of sessions. For instance the counsellor noted with Mr C that his arrogance reached a crescendo whenever he had shown any kind of vulnerability to the counsellor. This helped the counsellor understand his arrogance as a defence against feeling vulnerable.

Counter-transference

The counsellor not only observes what the client does and listens to both the content and process of what she says, he also registers the impact of the client on him. This impact on the counsellor might take the form of a bodily sensation, or the counsellor finding himself in a certain mood, or having feelings, thoughts or fantasies about the client. These reactions to the client are called the *counter-transference.* The counter-transference is the way the client's transference onto the counsellor resonates with him, allowing the counsellor to recognize the transference by the way it affects him.

The term 'counter-transference' has undergone a change of meaning in the history of psychoanalysis. Freud originally used the term to refer to the analyst's transference onto the patient, in other words the tendency on the therapist's part to re-enact with the patient his own pathological or unresolved object-relationships. In this sense counter-transference was seen as something to be suppressed or eliminated in the therapist to guard against the therapist acting out his transference feelings with the patient.

Although the term 'counter-transference' is still occasionally used in this way, it is now much more often used to refer to the impact on the therapist of the patient's transference. If the therapist or counsellor can allow himself to be open to this impact, to become aware of it and be able to think about its nature and meaning, then he will have a powerful way of apprehending the transference. In a classic paper on understanding counter-transference in this way, the psychoanalyst Paula Heimann noted how those starting out as analysts or therapists are often frightened of the feelings which are stirred up in them by their patients. 'If an analyst tries to work without consulting his feelings, his interpretations are poor. I have often seen this in the work of beginners, who, out of fear, ignored or stifled their feelings' (Heimann, 1950, p. 73). In such a case the beginning therapist will resort to their intellect in order to protect themselves against the emotional impact of the work with the patient. Trying to work without feelings involves getting rid of them as quickly as possible. But, said Heimann, if feelings can be sustained rather than discharged then they can be thought about and help the analyst understand more of the client.

Psychoanalytic work, according to Heimann has both an intellectual and an emotional component. The analyst uses his intellectual and cognitive abilities in order to listen to the patient and discern the allusions and implications of what the patient is saying. But there is another way of apprehending what the patient is communicating:

> I would suggest that the analyst along with this freely working attention needs a freely roused emotional sensibility so as to follow the patient's emotional movements and unconscious phantasies. Our basic assumption is that the analyst's unconscious understands that of his patient. This rapport on the deep level comes to the surface in the form of feelings which the analyst notices in response to his patient, in his 'counter-transference'. This is the most dynamic way in which his patient's voice reaches him. In the comparison of feelings roused in himself with his patient's associations and behaviour, the analyst possess[es] a most valuable means of checking whether he has understood or failed to understand his patient. (Heimann, 1950, p. 75)

Heimann here points to the great value of the analyst's 'freely roused emotional sensibility' as a way of tuning into the patient's unconscious communications. She also indicates that these counter-transference reactions on the part of the analyst need to be taken into account alongside the other available evidence from the patient, her associations and behaviour, against which the counter-transference can be checked.

In the case of Mrs A, the counsellor's freely roused emotional sensibility consisted, in part, of feelings of irritability concerning his client. These would be sparked off, for instance, when he would sometimes catch himself thinking that he might as well be part of the furniture for all the attention she seemed to pay to his comments to her. A few times he noticed his attention wandering while Mrs A was speaking, and he also noticed that on such occasions his thoughts might take him to another client, who was particularly grateful for the help she was receiving from him, or to a lecture he had recently given when his talk had been well received by the audience.

Now a counsellor who, as Heimann described, is frightened of having such thoughts or feelings about his client is likely to try to suppress them. But Mrs A's counsellor was sufficiently experienced to be able to be curious about the feelings and thoughts aroused in him by his work with Mrs A and to think of them as counter-transference reactions, stimulated in him by the transference relationship.

When he started to analyse his feelings and thoughts, the counsellor realized they were about feeling ignored by Mrs A and imagining compensatory situations in which his contributions were valued. He also noted that these counter-transference reactions occurred with greater frequency and intensity whenever Mrs A ignored or paid scant attention to his comments to her. He further realized that, by sometimes allowing his mind to wander when she was speaking, he was ignoring her just as she ignored him. Putting these reactions together he could see an object-relationship being enacted in the transference of one party being cold or indifferent towards the other party, who felt hurt and rejected. There was more evidence that this was the prevailing transference pattern from the content of the sessions, in that many of Mrs A's stories were of examples of how hurt she felt when people in her life did not understand her or take her seriously.

By being curious about his thoughts, feelings and fantasies aroused in him by the work, and thinking of them as a way of recognizing the transference, Mrs A's counsellor was less likely to act them out in the work. In other words the counsellor was able to contain his irritability, and, in fact, the more he could see his feeling as a form of communication from Mrs A about her own inner world, the less irritated he actually felt, and the less distracted he became in listening to Mrs A.

However it is not quite accurate to say that Mrs A's counsellor did not act out any of his counter-transference reactions. He had on occasions actually turned his attention away from Mrs A, that is, he had retaliated by dismissing her as she had dismissed him. This was a lapse on his part as he was unable to pay full attention to what she was saying. What this shows is that no counsellor can ever escape from the effect of the transference, he is bound to be affected by it, and therefore some acting out with the client is inevitable. But as long as such acting out is limited and recoverable, as it was with Mrs A's counsellor, such lapses can actually be of great value, for they allow the counsellor to recognize the transference by experiencing at first hand how it affects him and his conduct of the session (Carpy, 1989).

If the counsellor fails to see how he is caught in the transference, if he cannot register and think about his counter-transference reactions to the client, then his attitude and behaviour towards the client will solidify into what can be called a *counter-transference position* (Racker, 1985, pp. 142–6). The mark of a counsellor caught up in a counter-transference position is that he can think of the client in one way only, he is no longer free to use his imagination and sensibility to take up a different perspective. This was the case with Mr D's counsellor (see Chapter 5), who had to disregard any counter-transferential awareness of her anger, disappointment and resentment towards her client, which might have enabled her to recognize Mr D's negative transference towards her hidden behind his superficial compliance. The counsellor was stuck in a counter-transference position of trying only to think positively about the client, which resulted in the counselling making no progress and the client eventually leaving.

A counter-transference position is more likely with a client whose own thinking is inflexible. With an arrogant and contemptuous client like Mr C, for instance (see Chapter 5), the counsellor might all too easily adopt a corresponding combative or aggressive attitude towards the client. If this attitude on the counsellor's part solidifies into a counter-transference position, then a vicious circle will be set up, in which the counsellor's defensive/aggressive response to the client will further fuel his arrogance towards the counsellor, and so on. In such situations the counselling is likely to break down.

In order to avoid taking up a counter-transference position, and to think about the transference in general, the counsellor needs to learn to monitor his counter-transference reactions during the session. This presupposes an ability on the counsellor's part to discriminate between what has been projected into him by the client and what belongs to him. This can never be an exact distinction, for, as we have seen, what the client projects into the counsellor has to find some resonance from the counsellor's own make-up in order to take root. Furthermore, we can never be transparent to ourselves, so in trying to ascertain our own states of mind, some of which are more conscious than others, we are always to some extent groping in the dark. Nevertheless trying to think about the origins of our reactions to the client is still crucial in order to judge what thoughts and feelings are to count as counter-transference.

For example, how was Mrs A's counsellor to know that his feeling of irritation was a counter-transference reaction rather than something which had nothing to do with the client? Maybe the counsellor had had a row with a colleague that morning, or was simply in a bad mood that day and so came into the counselling session already predisposed to feel irritable. The counsellor needs to pay attention to feelings or reactions left over from previous encounters, which might get in the way of his ability to stay open to what the client brings. What is much more difficult to see are deeper influences on the way the counsellor responds to the client, to do with the counsellor's own personal history and the nature of his object-relations. In other words, what also has to be brought into the equation is the counsellor's transference onto the client (his counter-transference in the old sense of the word). What is crucial here is how far the counsellor knows about his own transference tendencies and vulnerabilities, and so can do his best to take account of them. The development of this capacity for self-analysis is an essential part in training to become a psychodynamic counsellor. It is fostered in the supervision of the counsellor's work, and above all in his own personal therapy which is part of his training.

In the case of Mrs A, for instance, the counsellor realized that Mrs A reminded him in some ways of his own mother, whom he had experienced when a boy, as someone who did not take enough notice of him. The counsellor could see he was therefore in more danger with that particular aspect of the transference of losing his sense of perspective. For example he might react to Mrs A being dismissive of him in the same way as he had responded to his mother as a child. However because he had explored his relationship with his mother in some depth in his own personal therapy, the counsellor felt he knew enough about this susceptibility on his part to confuse the client with his own mother in order to take account of it in his understanding of Mrs A.

What follows from this is that the client's transference onto the counsellor does not occur in a vacuum, it becomes a creation of both client and counsellor. Whatever transferences and object-relationships the client brings to the relationship, the counsellor brings his own valency for taking on certain projections or acting out certain roles. This jointly created transference can be thought of as a kind of 'double' of the counsellor (Green, 1972), a figure modelled on aspects of the counsellor as he is but shaped in accord with the client's transference. Nevertheless, although both client and counsellor contribute to the creation of this transference-figure, they do so in different ways. Whereas the client will invest heavily in this transference-figure, taking it to be the counsellor, the counsellor sets himself the task of de-constructing this jointly created figure, and thereby helping the client see her part in its creation.

Working in the transference

The ability to work in the transference is the most distinctive feature of the psychodynamic approach. Working in the transference means having an eye on the transference aspect of whatever is occurring in the session. So, for instance, if the client is speaking about the latest row with her husband/boss/sister, the counsellor might have in the back of her mind such thoughts as 'I wonder what the client is telling me about her experience of the counselling in this story?', or 'the client is describing a relationship between an angry and a frightened person, I wonder if this is also a reference to something happening in the transference?'

It is important to make a distinction between thinking in the transference and speaking directly of the transference to the client. An essential part of becoming a psychodynamic counsellor is the ability to think in the transference, that is pay attention to and try to understand the transference. Whether or not the counsellor then chooses to speak of the transference is determined by the current situation in the counselling. Having recognized the predominant form of transference in play, the counsellor may decide it does not need to be addressed, as we saw with Mrs A and the erotic transference. The counsellor may also decide that rather than directly address the transference with the client, he would do better to use his transference understanding to help him make more sense of the client's other relationships (Pearson, 1995). For example, if the counsellor sees the client enacting a sadomasochistic relationship with him, he might use this understanding to help the client see this feature in her marriage. This might be more productive with a client who would be likely to find direct transference interpretation bewildering or disturbing.

Another way of working with a client who might find it difficult to think of a relationship with the counsellor as a person would be to speak of the transference in terms of the counselling setting.

So the counsellor might speak of the effect of the 'counselling' on the client rather than couching things in terms of the client's relationship to himself (Balint, 1968). Such a way of speaking might be seen as a way of testing the water, a preliminary step towards making a more direct transference interpretation about the counsellor as a person.

Much of the skill in becoming a psychodynamic counsellor, and much of the development of one's own personal way of working will be in this area, of deciding whether, when and how to address the transference with each client. A more detailed discussion of these issues takes us beyond the scope of this introductory text, and is more properly the subject of the case discussion and supervision which is part of a counselling training. However a few general principles or rules of thumb can be given as an introductory guide in this area.

As a rule it is unwise to address the transference directly with a client whose thinking is at the level of symbolic equation, as he or she will not be able to distinguish between real and symbolic, wish and deed. The psychoanalyst Herbert Rosenfeld gives an example of this in his treatment of a young girl who had sexual delusions of people wanting to marry her.

> During the treatment the delusions could be seen very clearly within an Oedipal framework, and I interpreted her only too obvious incestuous sexual wishes in relation to me. For example, after she had told me that a voice had just told her that she was going to get married in a month's time I pointed out to her that she had begun to care for me and hoped that I would marry her. To my surprise these transference interpretations unfortunately made her very much worse; her delusions increased, and she had to go into a mental hospital for a long time. I felt very bad about this result, but it eventually helped me to realize that interpretations of openly Oedipal material were very dangerous in schizophrenia. This was an important discovery which eventually enabled me to formulate ideas about the concrete nature of psychotic thinking and feeling and its influence on the way the analyst's interpretations can be distorted so that they are misheard as actual suggestions. (Rosenfeld, 1987, p. 10)

Counsellors are unlikely, except in specialized settings, to come across clients as manifestly disturbed as this. However some clients do think at the level of symbolic equation (see Chapter 4), such as Ms F (see Chapter 5), who confused speaking about sex to the counsellor with having sex with him. For that reason her counsellor refrained from speaking directly about her sexual feelings for him, interpreting them as a wish on her part to get close to him. Only later in the counselling, when Ms F felt more contained, did she begin to distinguish symbol (word) from what it symbolized (the action of having sex), and thus be able to think about her sexual wishes regarding the counsellor without feeling compelled to act them out.

Some clients will indicate a readiness to explore the transference, for example by making direct references to the counsellor (as in Mr E's remarks to the counsellor about her clothes or his question as to whether she was married). In such instances the rule of thumb would be that the counsellor should accept this invitation to explore the transference, as the client would then be likely to interpret a failure of the counsellor to follow this up as a sign of his wish to avoid the transference. If the work has reached an impasse, or has become lifeless and predictable with no change in the client (as in the case of Mr D), this is a sign that some important feature of the transference is probably being acted out rather than addressed, and the counselling will not get going again until this has been explored and understood. If the client gets worse during the counselling (as Mrs A did around the time of the final break) then, again, this is likely to do with the transference, the turn for the worse probably being a sign of an unaddressed negative transference.

If the counselling is progressing satisfactorily, and the counsellor is paying proper attention to the setting, then there is no need to directly address the transference. However the counsellor might choose to interpret the transference in order to make more immediate contact with the client, or to more effectively address her anxiety. As a general rule, when the transference is addressed by the counsellor the client is likely to feel a mixture of anxiety and relief, anxiety as the stakes will be raised in the counselling which will now directly concern the relationship between client and counsellor, and relief that the counsellor is able to tolerate and directly address the impact the client is having on him.

We can illustrate some of the different ways the transference might be dealt with by the counsellor by returning to the case of the bulimic client Ms B (see Chapter 4). From the beginning the counsellor noticed that although Ms B always listened politely to what she might say in a session, it never seemed to make any difference to her. The counsellor also became aware that whatever state Ms B was in at the end of a session, by the next time they met she had totally regained her calm demeanour. Putting these observations together, the counsellor came to recognize that Ms B could take in little of what he said to her, and what she did take in was effectively got rid of by the time of the next session. In other words Ms B's bulimia was being enacted in the transference.

However at this early point in the work the counsellor did not feel she had established a strong enough working alliance with Ms B to speak directly of the transference to her, and that she might find such an interpretation invasive or controlling. In these early sessions Ms B was preoccupied with her relationship with her boy-friend, which seemed to be in danger of imminent collapse. The counsellor was able to use her understanding of the transference to help her identify a similar bulimic dynamic being played out in Ms B's relationship with her boyfriend, where he complained that she never listened to him, but she felt too scared that if she took in what he said to her then she would feel as if he were controlling her. Whenever this pattern was pointed out to her by the counsellor Ms B felt better able to tolerate the ups and downs in her relation-ship with her boyfriend.

At a later stage in the counselling, Ms B cancelled several sessions in a row. The counsellor then realized that the bulimic quality of the counselling relationship was now being acted out in a more ser-ious way and had to be directly addressed. In the session following her self-imposed break Ms B was in an excited and agitated state, flitting from topic to topic and unable to stay long enough with an issue to begin to reflect on it and what it might mean. She claimed to see no meaning in her absence beyond a need to take a break from the counselling, and saw no point in 'dwelling' on it. The counsellor felt she needed to try to establish a thinking space in the session, and that one way of doing that was to speak to Ms B directly about the transference, linking it directly to the cancelled sessions. The counsellor told Ms B that she was in constant fear of the counsellor's words getting inside her and contaminating her. That was why she had been absent, to get rid of those parts of the counsellor which she felt were taking her over, in the same way she had to expel her food when it became bad and threatened to attack the good things inside her. Ms B was at first indignant and took what the counsellor said as an attack. The counsellor responded to this by saying to Ms B that she had now turned the counsellor's interpretation, which offered her something potentially nourishing, into something hostile and invasive, from which she had to defend herself. She had done this, the counsellor continued, as Ms B felt attacked by the counsellor rather than understood. The counsellor had suddenly changed for her from being a good person into a bad one, just like her food in her stomach changed from being nourishing to poisonous. This now made sense to Ms B. She was able to concede that she had been anxious about returning, and was gradually able to acknowledge the bulimic relationship she had created with the counsellor.

This change in the quality of the counsellor, from being a good and nourishing object to a bad and dangerous one, took place again in the following session. Ms B had been telling the counsellor something to do with her boyfriend, and the counsellor made a comment a shade sharper than was usual. The effect on Ms B was dramatic: her face changed, and a flash of anger appeared in her eyes, before it vanished and was replaced by a cold and distant look. She then lapsed into silence. When the counsellor asked her what was wrong, Ms B said she no longer felt like talking, but was unable to say why. At this point the counsellor could see that Ms B had withdrawn in order to protect herself against some disturbing experience in the transference. The counsellor felt at this point the most containing response she could make was to address the transference in a way that would make direct and vivid contact with Ms B and her transference experience. So she said, 'a few moments ago I was a good and nourishing person for you, and now I have suddenly changed into a bad and harmful one. This change was so frightening and disturbing to you that you now have to distance yourself from me in order to protect yourself.' Ms B was struck by the directness of the counsellor's interpretation. She nodded and was silent for a few moments, but this time in a thoughtful rather than a distant way. She went on to speak of how this kind of thing would frequently happen with her mother, that she would be speaking animatedly to her mother about something, who was warm and responsive, and then suddenly her mother would freeze or become angry about something she (Ms B) had said and just walk out of the room, leaving Ms B feeling devastated and empty.

This example illustrates how the counsellor used her understanding of the transference in different ways. In the earlier part of the work the counsellor used the transference dimension to help Ms B make sense of a relationship outside of the counselling. At a later stage, with a more firmly established working alliance, the counsellor spoke directly to Ms B *about* the transference, that is the way in which Ms B was relating to the counsellor as though she was an invasive object which had to be expelled between sessions. This way of speaking was designed to create a reflective space in which joint exploration of the transference could take place. In the following session the counsellor felt it more important to make immediate and powerful contact with the client, to bring the transference alive, and she did this by speaking to the client *in* the transference. That is, the counsellor spoke as though she were the transference figure in question ('before I was a good person for you and now I have changed into a bad one'). Reality-testing, that is helping the client see that the counsellor had at this point become confused with some significant figure or internal object of the client, could come later. And, indeed, once Ms B heard her transference experience articulated by the counsellor, she was able to remember a series of incidents with her mother which threw light on the origins of the transference relationship in play with the counsellor.

This is the point of addressing the transference with the client, to open up new layers or lines of enquiry or unblock those that have become stuck. Interventions which are transference-based are the most powerful at the counsellor's disposal, as they bring the client's conflicts and object-relationships to life. They do this in a way which brings the counselling relationship itself into the area of mutual exploration, and thus add a new dimension to the client's experience.

Summary

The most distinctive feature of psychodynamic counselling is the attention paid to the transference. Transference is a form of projection in which the client transfers aspects of significant figures and relationships onto the counsellor, and thereby experiences the counsellor as if he embodies these attributes or as though he is playing out the object-relationship with the client. Transference can be seen as the way parts of the objects and object-relationships which make up the client's internal world become enacted in the relationship with the counsellor.

The client's positive transference to the counsellor, seeing him as a benign and helpful figure, forms the basis for the working alliance, which enables the client to become engaged in the counselling and continue working in the face of the difficulties and frustrations that will inevitably be encountered. The positive transference is the counsellor's ally in managing the negative transference, in which the counsellor will be experienced as an untrustworthy, useless or malevolent figure. Another form of transference is the erotic transference, when the client falls in love with the counsellor and experiences him as the object of her sexual desire. Transference is a form of repetition in which the client enacts aspects of her previous relationships. However the repetition is never exact. There is also something new in the transference relationship, in which the client gives expression to feelings or thoughts which have hitherto been repressed. As well as these different forms of transference, which are based on the client's individual and family history, the counsellor needs to keep in mind the social dimension of the transference, in which aspects of the client's cultural and ethnic identity will find expression in the counselling relationship.

The counsellor looks for evidence of the transference from three main sources: the way the client conducts herself in the sessions, what she says and how it is said, and the counsellor's reactions to the client and his work with her. This last feature is called the counter-transference. Learning to monitor and think about the counter-transference requires both experience and self-knowledge on the part of the counsellor, normally acquired through supervision and the counsellor's own therapy. The counsellor works in the transference by trying to ascertain the prevailing transference pattern at any given time in the counselling. Having recognized the transference, the counsellor may then decide to speak to the client about the transference. This issue of whether, when and how to speak of the transference to the client is really a subject for training and supervision. But a few general guidelines can be given, for instance if the counselling has got stuck or the client is getting worse, this is a sign that something about the transference has not been addressed.

Further reading

Hollands, D (2004) 'Reflections on client-counsellor communication', *Psychodynamic Practice*, vol. 10, no. 4, pp. 490–9.

Holmes, G and Perrin, A (1997) 'Countertransference: what it is? What do we do with it?', *Psychodynamic Practice*, vol. 3, no. 3, pp. 263–78.

Malan, D (1979) *Individual Psychotherapy and the Science of Psychodynamics*, London: Butterworths (especially ch. 9 'The relationship with the therapist: transference' and ch. 10 'The dialogue of psychotherapy and the two triangles').

Racker, H (1985) *Transference and Counter-transference*, London: Maresfield Library.

Rouholamin, C (2007) 'The 'frame' as a container for the erotic transference – a case study, *Psychodynamic Practice*, vol. 13, no. 2, pp. 181–96.

7

PHASES OF
THE COUNSELLING WORK

As a counsellor, one never knows in advance what any session with a client will throw up. Nevertheless it is possible to identify some typical characteristics and rhythms of the different phases of the work which can help the counsellor provide a context for understanding what happens with the client. Suppose, for instance, that the client starts to come late for sessions. What this means will be specific to each client. However the lateness may also be a communication about the particular stage reached in the work as a whole. If it occurs in the beginning phase, when the therapeutic alliance is not yet well established, the lateness may be a sign that the counselling setting may not yet be experienced by the client as secure. In the middle period the work usually starts to become consolidated. But now the client's lateness may herald a crisis in the work, particularly concerning the transference as the client's particular difficulties become more clearly enacted in the counselling. As the ending of the counselling comes into view, the emphasis is likely to shift towards how the client will deal with the termination of the work, and what can be carried over into the client's life after counselling. This may indicate another way the client's lateness can be understood: now not so much about being able to trust the counsellor (the beginning phase) or the repetition of past disappointments and conflicts (the middle phase) but a loss of faith in whether what has been good about the counselling can survive the turmoil of the ending.

The beginning phase

For many counsellors the first contact with a client will be at the first appointment made for the client to begin counselling. However before she has set eyes on the counsellor, the client will already have a history with the agency or institution involved, and this will have a bearing on the beginning of the counselling proper. There will have been a *referral* made to the agency or institution in which the counsellor is working, and some process of *assessment* in which it was decided that counselling was appropriate for the client.

Referral

Whether or not the counsellor was directly involved in the referral, the way the client finds her way into the agency or organization where the counselling takes place will make its mark on the future work. Of particular importance here is, first, whether the client really wants counselling, and, second, whether the client has a realistic understanding of what counselling entails. Consider the following example.

A counselling agency received the following letter from a local GP: 'I hope you will accept Mrs X as an urgent referral. This unfortunate woman has been the subject of an extended investigation by Social Services concerning her care of her two children, and has come to see me in a very distressed state, saying she feels so depressed she does not feel she can go on.' The letter went on to give some factual information about Mrs X and her family (ages, husband), and to say that a low dose of anti-depressive medication was being prescribed. The letter ended by reiterating that Mrs X felt desperate, and was expecting a letter soon from the counselling agency.

There is no doubt, from this referral letter, that here is a client in a lot of distress. But the problem is that it is not clear who is really seeking help. We know that the doctor is in a fix, probably in having had to manage a difficult consultation and feeling under pressure to come up with some avenue of help for his patient to follow, but we are left in the dark as to whether Mrs X herself wants counselling or is interested in or capable of the self-reflection that counselling necessarily entails. It may be that there is an unrealistic expectation about counselling, namely the idea that if Mrs X were to seek counselling, she would be more likely to get her children back from Social Services. It is clear that if these issues are not clarified – whether by speaking to the GP, or by inviting Mrs X in for an assessment – any future counselling work will be undertaken on the basis of confusion or misunderstanding.

Such ambiguities around who is really seeking help for what can arise not only in third-party referrals, as in this example, but also in self-referrals.

*A client who had approach a counselling agency for help wrote the following
in his questionnaire as to why he was seeking counselling: 'I have come to
the painful realization that I am addicted to online gambling. I have made
huge losses and am no longer able to pay the mortgage. My wife is very
upset and is threatening to leave with the children unless I get help. The
situation is desperate and I don't know where to turn'.*

Clearly, as in the previous example, the client is in a desperate situation, and it may seem hard to turn someone away from seeking
counselling who is in dire straits. It may indeed be for this man that
his 'painful realization' is the start of some serious self-reflection,
which could form the basis for some productive counselling work.
But it may also be that the prime motive for seeking counselling
is to gain ammunition in his battle to stop his wife leaving him,
coupled with an unrealistic expectation that counselling will 'cure'
him of his addiction. If such a client were to start work without such
expectations having been addressed, the work is unlikely to prove
of benefit.

Even where referrals seem much more straight-forward, with
a client clearly seeking relief from their suffering through self-
understanding and self-exploration, there needs to be some form
of *assessment*, a consultation with the client as to whether a psychological intervention of some kind will be of help, and, if so, whether
counselling is the most appropriate.

Assessment

In most counselling or therapy organizations a client who first seeks
help will be offered an assessment meeting. Once the assessment is
completed, the assessor will normally pass on the client to one of his
colleagues, who will be the one who does the counselling work. The
purpose of the assessment meeting is for counsellor and client to
gain an overview of the client's difficulties, and then consider how
best to respond to them.

Carrying out a psychodynamic assessment involves the same
skills as in the normal work of counselling, but in a much more concentrated form as the time-frame for an assessment is usually one or
perhaps two sessions. Doing an assessment is not just a question of
history-taking, although gathering the most relevant aspects of the
client's history and present circumstances is important. A psychodynamic assessment is a much more active process in which counsellor and client try to think together about the nature of the client's

problems, whether psychodynamic counselling is likely to be of benefit, and, if it is, whether the client will be able to cope with the feelings, states of mind and conflicts which may well arise as a consequence of the work. The counsellor will also need to manage the assessment session or sessions so that any issues which have arisen during the assessment, particularly concerning the transference, have been sufficiently addressed for the client to move on, whether to a period of counselling in the agency with another worker, or to some other form of intervention, or whether the client decides that the consultation itself has been sufficient for the time being (see Malan, 1979, pp. 209–53 for further elaboration of these aspects of the assessment process).

The following example illustrates some of these issues.

Mr G referred himself for counselling saying he had recently become depressed. He met with a (male) counsellor for an assessment meeting, and spoke with feeling about a number of recent setbacks in both his work and personal life, and how he now found himself subject to black moods which could be so severe that on occasions he could not get out of bed in the mornings. He had several failed relationships with women, and was despondent about ever being in a relationship that worked. He responded well to the counsellor's comments, and was able spontaneously to link his present difficulties with his childhood experiences of being with a distant and overworked father, and a mother with whom he was still very close but never felt she was strong enough for him to tell her what he was really feeling. Mr G talked about his relief in finally seeking counselling, having put off seeking help at several difficult periods in his life. The counsellor found Mr G engaging, articulate, insightful and motivated, and felt sure that counselling could help him.

The assessing counsellor's normal practice was to have two assessment sessions with his clients, and Mr G was happy to come back for a second meeting. This session began with Mr G saying how helpful he had found the first meeting with the counsellor, and he said again how relieved he was that he was now taking some action. This seemed a good sign for future work, that he was able to make use of a psychodynamic approach as he had found the first assessment session helpful, and that he had no adverse reactions to the first meeting, such as being plunged back into his depression, which might have been a warning that counselling might make him worse rather than better. The counsellor asked Mr G to say more about what had been helpful about their first meeting. Mr G gave a rather vague reply, and, on being asked by the counsellor to elaborate, could only repeat that he had made the first step. This was not what the counsellor had expected, and he now found himself unsure as to how to proceed. A little later in the session the same thing happened. The counsellor had returned to Mr G's relationship with his mother, and asked Mr G what he had meant when he had described his relationship with mother as being 'close', when he felt unable to confide in her about how depressed he often felt. Again Mr G seemed nonplussed, described more ways in which he felt close to his mother, and finally said that he did not know what the counsellor was getting at. Mr G now started to look disconcerted and the counsellor felt disoriented and stuck.

A less experienced or confident counsellor might have taken Mr G's evident discomfort as a signal for him to back off at this point. However the counsellor knew that Mr G's anxiety at this point needed to be explored and understood rather than suppressed, which would only have ended up repeating the kind of relationship that Mr G had with his mother. The counsellor felt an interpretation here would be the best way forward, and he spoke to Mr G about how the very problem he had come with, feeling demoralized and stuck in relationships, was now happening before their very eyes. Mr G could only agree with this, and in fact this intervention allowed him to speak with more feeling about his sense that he lacked the resources to sustain a proper relationship. The counsellor invited Mr G to speak more, and, rather reluctantly, he started to talk about his most recent relationship, which had ended when his girlfriend complained that she thought he had no real feelings for her. Mr G then went on to acknowledge that he, too, sometimes doubted whether any of his feelings or thoughts were real, or whether they had simply been copied from other people. He added, 'thinking like this really scares me, as I then start to think that I am going mad'.

Time was now running out, and the counsellor returned to the question as to whether Mr G still wanted counselling. Mr G said he did, but he could now see that entering counselling would mean bringing up his deepest fears about himself, and he wondered how he would cope with this, and also where this would leave him when the counselling ended. The final part of the assessment session was taken up in an exploration of these questions, which were a sign of Mr G's more realistic appreciation of what was involved in counselling. Whereas earlier in this session the counsellor had started to wonder whether Mr G was robust enough to manage an exploration of his feelings, his ability to respond well to the counsellor's intervention was now evidence that he did seem to have the resources necessary to benefit from counselling.

This example illustrates that the best guide for an assessing counsellor as to whether psychodynamic work is appropriate is to give the client an experience of the work itself, in this case by giving Mr G an interpretation about his getting stuck and demoralized in the session, and then seeing whether the client can make use of this intervention. Mr G was able to respond by exploring his anxiety further, and this led on to a more realistic sense of how he would probably cope with counselling.

Much more could be said about this assessment in particular and assessment in general (see Spurling, 2003 for further discussion, and for a list of useful references). What we want to draw attention to here is that, whatever the outcome of the assessment, there will be consequences of the first meeting with the counsellor. Suppose the assessor, instead of exploring Mr G's feelings when he became stuck, had instead backed off at that point. Given Mr G's motivation and readiness for counselling, it is likely that he would still have been offered counselling. But now he would have been coming to the first meeting with a new counsellor not having had his fears contained, in fact having had his expectation unwittingly confirmed by the assessor that his feelings were too much for anyone else to bear, and so likely unconsciously to expect the same from the new counsellor.

The first session and the beginning phase

The first session marks the start of the beginning phase of the work. The main task of this phase of the counselling is to enable the client to become engaged in the work. In other words, the counsellor will be working towards establishing or laying the ground for a *working alliance* to develop (see p. 97), that is the identification of a capacity on the client's part to reflect on her behaviour and to speak to the counsellor about her reflections. It is this dialogue between the counsellor and that part of the client that can think and reflect, which will sustain the rest of the work.

In the *first session* the counsellor aims to get the counselling underway. One task of this first meeting is to decide with the client on the nature of the counselling contract, that is, the details of frequency of sessions, over what period of time, and where the counselling will take place (see pp. 28–31). However, before this can be fruitfully negotiated the counsellor needs to get a sense of the client's readiness to start the counselling. A good way to judge this is to hear from the client how they have arrived at this first meeting, that is an account of the client's particular history with the agency or organization in which the counsellor is working. As we have seen with Mr G, a crucial part of this would be to hear about the client's experience of the assessment, because there may well be unfinished business which needs to be addressed. Furthermore, the client's experience of the assessment, and of all previous experiences of counselling or therapy, can provide valuable clues as to what may lie ahead in the counselling work.

Ms H was a woman in her early thirties who had come for counselling following a period of depression. In the first meeting with her (female) counsellor, when asked about her assessment in the counselling agency, she spoke of her strong reaction to something the (male) assessor had said to her, which had been playing on her mind. She had been telling him about a previous relationship which had broken down, and the counsellor had remarked on the fact that she seemed to find ways of keeping her boyfriend at bay. Ms H said she had felt extremely put out by this comment, which she felt misrepresented what she had been saying, and had argued with the counsellor. Although she had found the assessment session of value overall, this had been her strongest impression of the meeting.

The counsellor asked for clarification about this incident: what had Ms H felt when the counsellor had spoken, how did she come to the conclusion that it was a misrepresentation, were she and the assessing counsellor able to talk about what had happened? Ms H was unable to say much more, beyond saying that she had felt very angry with the counsellor, that he had twisted what she had said, and that they were not able to resolve the issue in the meeting.

This event with the assessing counsellor did not seem to affect Ms H's readiness to start the counselling proper, and in the first few sessions with the new counsellor she seemed able to talk openly about her difficulties. But in the fifth session, after the counsellor had made a comment about how Ms H might be feeling after an argument she had described with her boss at work, Ms H reacted sharply, saying to the counsellor 'you are putting words into my mouth'. Some tense interchanges followed, with the counsellor struggling to understand why what she had said on this occasion, which seemed to her no different in either tone or content to many other remarks she had made in the previous sessions, had had such an effect on Ms H. For her part, Ms H wanted to know what was in the counsellor's mind when she had made the remark, and how could the counsellor know what she might be feeling. Further exploration led to Ms H feeling slightly calmer by the time the session ended.

In the next session Ms H was able to make an important link. She said she had been thinking about what had happened in the previous session, and she could now see that what she had been feeling with the counsellor reminded her of how she had often felt with her mother when she was growing up. Ms H often felt hurt by the way her mother would criticize her for the way she talked or dressed, making clear her disappointment in her daughter for not thinking or behaving in the way she (mother) felt was right for an ado-lescent girl. This had affected Ms H so powerfully as a teenager that she had resolved never to confide in her mother again. Further discussion of her relationship with her mother enabled Ms H to see even more clearly that something of what she remembered feeling when criticized by her mother – a potent and confusing mix of rage, despair, and a powerful sense of having been intruded upon and misrepresented – had been reactivated in the previ-ous counselling session, and, indeed, also in the assessment.

Further incidents of this kind continued over the course of the counsel-ling (which lasted one year). Every time Ms H was able to talk about these experiences with the counsellor, and see how they could be both tolerated and understood in the session, her ability to trust the counsellor and coun-selling increased.

Here we can get a glimpse of how a working alliance gets estab-lished. An experience of being understood by the counsellor is an essential part of this. The counsellor did not defend herself when Ms H accused her of putting words into her mouth, which would probably have been experienced by Ms H as the counsellor not lis-tening to her (as she felt her mother had not listened to her). Neither, however, did the counsellor simply agree with the complaint. Instead the counsellor's attitude of curiosity and a wish to make sense of what was happening enabled Ms H to arrive at a piece of under-standing herself. It is often the case that it takes an experience of *misunderstanding*, and then having the occasion of misunderstand-ing explored and made sense of, that the client comes to have a more robust sense of working together with the counsellor. An important ingredient is the idea of *repair*, that the inevitable conflicts, tensions and misunderstandings that will arise with the counsellor in the course of the work can be spoken about, and to a sufficient extent made tolerable or even resolved.

Sometimes, however, what appears to be the establishment of a working alliance with a client may turn out to be something else.

A (female) counsellor had been working with a (female) client, Ms I, for about three months. The client had asked for counselling because of periods of severe depression. In the initial period in the counselling Ms I reported that the depression she had initially complained of seemed to have lifted, and she spoke of starting to enjoy her life again. However she then started com-ing to sessions complaining of a lack of energy, of difficulties in her relation-ships, of not getting to sleep – all the symptoms of depression which now seemed to be returning. The counsellor helped the client explore these feel-ings, and this seemed to bring a little relief. The counsellor was also able to

link the client's depression to events in the counselling, such as an impending break, and this also made sense to Ms I. The counsellor felt it important
to keep alive the client's sense of hope, that her depression could be tolerated,
and tried to focus on the way Ms I would habitually dismiss or undermine
her own resources, for example by constantly belittling herself, which again
seemed to help the client gain a useful perspective on herself.

Nevertheless Ms I continued to come to sessions feeling depressed, and
the counsellor gradually came to notice that she was starting to feel rather
demoralized herself, no longer looking forward to sessions with this client as
she had done when the work started, and even finding it hard to remember
what had happened in the sessions after they had finished.

When the counsellor was able to reflect on what was going on, a process
helped by taking the case to supervision, she came to see that she did not
really want to hear about Ms I's very depressed feelings, as they left her
feeling helpless and useless. She was sure that the client was picking this
up, which, the counsellor now realized, must have left Ms I feeling that her
depressed feelings were truly unbearable, and that the counsellor was only
interested in hearing about her happy or resourceful side. This would in all
likelihood only increase her feelings of depression – precisely what the client
seemed to be unconsciously communicating in continuously bringing her
symptoms of depression to the counsellor.

Once the counsellor realized this, she was able to change her attitude
towards Ms I. Instead of mentally turning away when Ms I again complained about feeling too tired to do anything, or being unable to sleep,
the counsellor allowed herself to become curious about these states of
mind, and to actively encourage the client to explore them in more depth.
Initially this felt risky to the counsellor, as though she was inviting Ms I
to plunge deeper into the depression. However Ms I responded well to
this change of attitude, saying that never before had she felt safe enough
to really look at these awful states. Over time this marked an important
shift in the client's attitude towards her depression. Rather than seeing
it as a state of mind to be avoided and feared, she gradually came to see
her depression as a kind of constant companion, a state of mind she knew
she would fall in to from time to time, but which could be survived and
tolerated.

In this example it was the counsellor's ability to free herself from
a counter-transference position (see p. 114) of feeling bored and
demoralized that in turn allowed the client to take a significant step
forward: to no longer flee from her depression as an unbearable
state to be avoided at all costs, to gradually and painfully accepting
it as a part of herself, albeit an ill or sick part. Instead of being stuck

in a cycle of complaint by the client met by ineffectual reassurance by the counsellor, the work was able to take on shape and focus as a working alliance was established which now had depth and solidity. This could be described as the proper beginning of the counselling – although no doubt the hard work put in by both counsellor and client up to that point in trying to make sense of the client's feelings lay the ground for this development.

The middle phase

As we have seen from the previous example, the distinction between the beginning and middle phase of counselling can seem artificial, as it may take a long time for a good enough working alliance to be established, and with some very disturbed clients the working alliance may always feel precarious (see the examples of Mr K and Mr L in the next chapter). If the work has got off to a good enough start, the middle phase of the work may sometimes be felt to begin with the first crisis in the work. The most characteristic aspects of the middle phase of the work are to do with *depth* and with *consolidation*. It is typically in this phase that the changes that have already taken place in the beginning phase can be explored in more depth. Formerly hidden or buried feelings, thoughts and memories are more likely to surface, with the consequence that the client may, for the first time, be able to speak of what had hitherto been too difficult or frightening to verbalize. For example with Mrs A (see p. 41) it was her reaction to the first holiday break in the counselling – an important event which often marks a shift from the beginning to the middle phase – which enabled her get in touch with her anger, and so begin to access with more depth her ambivalent feelings over her mother's death. With the establishment of a working alliance, these new developments can become consolidated as part of an expanding sense of self-mastery.

With the experiences of depth and consolidation there is often more of a sense of focus in the counselling, for example the need to understand a key relationship.

In this phase of the work Ms H, (see above p. 129) was able to explore in more depth and complexity her current relationship. This meant having to face up to feelings of competitiveness and envy in herself, states of mind hitherto denied. As she was increasingly able to acknowledge these feelings, Ms H was able to gain a different perspective on the rows she sometimes had with her boyfriend, and, for the first time, to discover that such rows were survivable. This important development was a consequence of Ms H first having had the experience with the counsellor that difficulties in their relationship could be repaired.

Nevertheless Ms H found disconcerting and bewildering any linking by the counsellor of her increasing ability to tolerate conflict and dissension with her boyfriend to what was happening in the counselling relationship. The old fear of misrepresentation, which on further exploration was closely linked to a fear of being intruded upon and controlled by the counsellor, tended to re-surface whenever the counsellor brought up the transference relationship, leaving Ms H feeling trapped rather than freed up by such interventions. Consequently the counsellor, while continuing to keep open the transference dimension of the work in her thinking, came to see that Ms H needed to keep the counsellor at a safe enough distance in order to use the counselling, and this precluded speaking directly to her of the transference relationship, except where Ms H herself could make a clear link.

This is an example of work where the counsellor used her understanding of the transference to help Ms H better understand her relationships outside of the consulting room (see p. 116). With many clients, however, the middle phase of the work is characterized by an opening up of the transference relationship itself, which is a consequence of the strengthening of the working alliance, and which also leads to a deepening sense of trust in the counsellor.

With Ms I (see above p. 130), now the working alliance had become more firmly established, the counsellor was able to help Ms I make more sense of both the structure of her depressed feelings, and some of the measures she took to evade them. When they explored her constant feelings of worthlessness, the counsellor pointed out to Ms I that she spoke as though she was constantly comparing herself to an ideal object or person, whose standards of perfection, beauty and intelligence she could never hope to meet. This made sense to Ms I, and she could now identify how crushed she often felt in the presence of other people, and how she feared their negative judgements on herself. The counsellor helped Ms I see how, in the counselling, she conducted herself in a similar way, justifying herself to the counsellor as though she expected her criticism. It then became possible for Ms I to explore this judging and critical person, whom she took the counsellor to be, as a projection of part of herself, the part that was constantly berating her for never being as good as the ideal object. In other words what became evident was how Ms I had transferred her own highly critical super-ego onto the figure of the counsellor.

Through exploring the counselling relationship Ms I also came to see how she habitually tried to evade this depressive cycle of feeling crushed by her super-ego. Ms I would sometimes come to sessions saying she felt much better, even happy, and proceeded to recount stories all of which seemed to illustrate this state of mind which was a very welcome relief to her depression, and gave her a sense of hope for the future. But when the counsellor gently pressed her to say more about this state of mind, she became reluctant to explore it, and when the counsellor then invited her to explore her reluctance, Ms I began to realize how superficial this state of mind was, and how easily it could vanish and leave her feeling once more heavy and depressed. In other words, she increasingly became able to distinguish states of real happiness – which she could feel, but usually only fleetingly – from manic states, which served as a flight from her depression. This allowed her to gain an idea of hope that was not based on a denial of depression, but on a way of coming to terms with it in a new way.

Here we can get a glimpse of the process of consolidation. Counsellor and client go over the same process – here exploring Ms I's depressive feelings and identifying her characteristic defences – but with an increasing sense of understanding leading to acceptance and even a sense of mastery. This can lead to the emergence of a sense of *hope.* The psychoanalyst Harold Searles comments on what he calls the development of mature hope as follows:

A healthy capacity for hope is founded, quite in contrast to a manic denial of depression, in past experiences of the successful integrating of disappointments – past experiences, that is, of successful grieving. Hope emerges through the facing of feelings of disappointment, discouragement and despair.

... hope comes into being when one discovers that such feelings as disappointment and despair can be shared with a fellow human being – when one discovers, that is, that the sharing of such feelings can foster one's feelings of relatedness with one's fellow human beings, rather than stigmatizing one as something less than human, something alien and unqualified to be included among human beings. (1979, p. 484)

The end phase

It is a distinctive feature of all kinds of therapy that both counsellor and client know that at some point the work will come to an end. In the beginning phase, even though in time-limited counselling the client will know when the work is scheduled to end, the termination date may still seem too far off to be of concern to her. The middle phase of the work is sometimes ushered in by a sense that the ending is now starting to come into view, and this fact may have a strong influence on what happens in this phase. However it is not until the ending becomes a primary feature of the work that we can speak of the end phase of the work.

The end phase is often dominated by an anxiety, whether articulated or not, as to whether the client will be able to manage her life once the counselling has come to an end. This anxiety can affect the work so powerfully that both client and counsellor can become convinced that a good ending in counselling means keeping the focus on the positive, for fear that exploring the client's disappointments or regrets about the counselling will spoil her confidence in her own resources to cope, or even thrive, after the ending of the counselling. But experience in managing endings in psychoanalytic work highlights the importance of giving the patient the experience of expressing and working through negative as well as positive feelings. So Melanie Klein in a classic paper entitled 'On the Criteria for the Termination of a Psycho-Analysis' commented:

> Good objects – as distinct from idealized ones – can be securely established in the mind only if the strong split between persecutory and ideal figures has diminished, if aggressive and libidinal impulses have come closer together, and hatred has become mitigated by love. (1950, p. 43)

In the following example we can see how difficult this process can be.

Ms J was approaching the end of two years of counselling, in which she felt a lot of good work had been done. A woman in her mid fifties, Ms J had come for help as she felt an underlying loneliness and misery, due, she thought, to the fact that she had never married and been unable to sustain any long relationship. After a year of counselling, she started a new relationship with a man, which seemed to go well. Nevertheless she often compared her new partner unfavourably with her (male) counsellor, commenting on how the counsellor understood her in a way her new partner never could. The counsellor was aware that a rather idealized transference relationship had developed, but attempts on his part to dismantle it by speaking of her idealization of him brought about no real shift in her expressed feelings for him, which continued to be primarily ones of admiration and gratitude.

As the ending date approached Ms J became more and more agitated about how she was going to cope without the support of the counsellor. She recognized that she had become dependent on the counsellor and, despite the fact

*that she was now in a relationship and that consequently her life was con-
siderably richer than when she had started counselling, she feared that she
could not sustain her new relationship without the counsellor's continuing
support. The counsellor did his best to encourage Ms J to explore the feelings
of loss, disappointment and abandonment. She was able to acknowledge that
she felt about the ending of the counselling, but she could not explore these
feelings with any real conviction or depth, and the counsellor continued to
the end to be an idealized figure for her.*

*About two years after the end of the counselling, Ms J contacted the coun-
selling agency again, to say that her feelings of misery and loneliness had
come back, and asked whether she could have some more sessions. She was
able to see the counsellor she had worked with before, and in their first session told him that for a time after the end of the counselling she had felt
much better about herself, but gradually she started to feel more and more
miserable. She was still with the man she had started the relationship with,
but they had nearly split up several times, and she now felt she was only
staying with him because she dreaded being alone again. She confided to the
counsellor that she often thought fondly of him, and told him how much she
missed having his support.*

*The counsellor said to Ms J that she had continued to hold onto an ideal-
ized image of him, and this had prevented her from ending properly and so
being able to make use of the counselling. Ms J acknowledged that she could
see this much more clearly now. The counsellor proposed they meet for a
further 12 sessions to see whether Ms J could reach a more satisfactory ending to their work.*

*As Ms J was now more receptive to recognizing and exploring her ideal-
ization of the counsellor, she began to realize how she split off any negative
feelings she might have towards the counsellor and located them in her partner. Then on one occasion the counsellor had to cancel a session at short
notice, and he forgot to tell Ms J about this. Consequently she turned up for
the session to find the counsellor was not there. At the next session she was
outraged that the counsellor clearly thought so little about her that he had
forgotten to tell her and, for the first time, launched into a critique of his
work with her. She said that whatever faults her partner had, and there were
many, he would never be so thoughtless as to forget to tell her about something he had to cancel. Towards the end of this session she calmed down
and, taken by surprise by the vehemence of her outburst against the counsellor, she started to back-track, saying she was sure the counsellor must have
had good reason to forget her. However the counsellor helped her see that
this retreat on her part was a consequence of her own guilt and fear about
expressing aggression towards him. Ms J left the session having astonished
herself with the depth of her critical feelings towards the counsellor, and*

felt this session had marked a breakthrough. In subsequent sessions she recounted her surprise at finding that her partner seemed to have suddenly become more understanding towards her, and consequently more lovable. Ms J now felt, for the first time, that she could sustain her relationship with her boyfriend, and as a consequence of her outburst towards the counsellor that something had been settled in the counselling. She now felt that she understood what it meant to have a proper ending to the counselling. After the termination of this additional piece of work, Ms J made no further contact with the agency.

This example is an exception to the normal situation where neither counsellor nor client can know what will happen once the counselling ends. This is because the end phase is no more than the culmination of the work that has gone on throughout the previous phases, that is the bringing together of hitherto split-off parts of the personality, and what might actually emerge from this new mix may well not have acquired shape or form by the end of the counselling. It is also because the client needs time to consolidate what she has experienced in the work. This can lead some to think of the period directly *after* the termination as the most crucial:

> I try to base my own technique on one cardinal assumption. This is that psychoanalysis is a long process in which what happens after the patient has left the psychoanalyst's consulting room for the last time is more important than what happens during the analysis. (Klauber, 1986, p. xvi)

For Ms J, despite the resurgence of her old problems, there seems to have been sufficient working-through since the end of the counselling for her to make good use of the opportunity given for a second bite of the cherry. But even with Ms J more open to trying to bring together her positive and negative feelings, it took a bit of acting out by the counsellor in forgetting to tell Ms J about a cancelled session to mobilize her feelings of disappointment and rage, and so give her an experience of 'hatred mitigated by love'. Consequently she was able to arrive at an ending which felt both tolerable and personal. In the first period of counselling the anxieties around loss inevitably stirred up by the ending felt so intense that it seemed to Ms J that only an idealized image of the counsellor could carry her over the ending of the counselling. For his part, as the counsellor realized in hindsight, he had been so affected by a sense of guilt that he was damaging the client in ending the counselling with her, that despite his best intentions he had been no more than half-hearted in trying to keep the focus on the negative aspects of the transference.

Normally clients do not have a second chance. Even if an agency is able to offer a follow-up session, it is unlikely there would be the resources for the client to have a further period of work. But even with her second chance, the example of Ms J shows how strong the wish can be, in both client and counsellor, to avoid the complex and painful feelings stirred up and issues raised by the ending of the counselling.

With Ms J her anxiety about the ending, and her primary defence of idealization as a way of avoiding persecutory feelings, were evident. But sometimes events seem to conspire to keep the focus of the work away from addressing the burning issue of the ending.

Ms H (see p. 129) never found it easy to talk about the counselling relationship itself, and seemed particularly reluctant to think about the ending. When they reached the half way stage of their one year contract, the counsellor reminded Ms H about the date of the ending, and as the ending date drew nearer she made more and more references to this event. However Ms H continued to remain preoccupied with her current relationship and found it hard to engage with the idea of an impending ending. By the tenth month, with two months to go until the planned end date, Ms H still reported she found talking about the ending unreal, although was able to be a little curious about the fact it seemed hard for her to take the ending seriously. Then, at the end of the tenth month, she reported a major crisis in her relationship with her boyfriend, when an ex-girlfriend of his made contact with him. Despite all her boyfriend's reassurances that this ex-partner now meant nothing to him, Ms H found herself consumed with feelings of jealousy, rage and insecurity.

The intensity of Ms H's feelings about this situation surprised both client and counsellor. Ms H was able to see that her fears were groundless, there was nothing in what her boyfriend said or did which suggested he wanted to get back together with his ex fiancée – yet she was unable to free herself from her persistent feeling that this now spelt the end of their relationship. With her increased anxiety and insistent questioning of her boyfriend about this previous relationship, it seemed for a time that Ms H might bring about what she most feared, that is actually push her boyfriend into turning away from her, which then might be used as a reason for leaving the relationship.

The counsellor was sure that this crisis encapsulated the most powerful feelings and fears that Ms H held about the ending of the counselling, which were now reaching a crescendo. But invitations to Ms H to explore these parallels, together with more direct interpretations by the counsellor that this crisis in her relationship with her boyfriend was a way of dealing with feelings about the ending of the counselling which she could not manage, fell on deaf ears. Ms H was intelligent enough to acknowledge that such interpretations sounded reasonable, and may well be correct, but in her frenzy of feeling about her boyfriend she could not connect to them or make anything of them.

As it became clear to the counsellor that Ms H's anxieties about the ending were too intense to be directly addressed at this point, she realized that only by exploring the new development with her boyfriend in more depth might Ms H find a way to gaining access to her feelings about the ending of the counselling. This is in fact what happened. Ms H found relief in talking to the counsellor about her jealousy of the ex-girlfriend, and as the ending drew even nearer the crisis with the boyfriend started to fade into the background. In the final two or three sessions Ms H was finally able to voice her fears about the ending of the counselling: how would she cope once the counselling had come to an end? The articulation of this anxiety now enabled the counsellor to make some links to the transference. She reminded Ms H that what had come up in her relationship with her boyfriend, namely feelings of competitiveness and jealousy, were what had sparked off her strong feelings of antipathy in her initial assessment, and early on in the counselling, and this allowed Ms H to review how she was now more able to acknowledge such feelings in herself without feeling too vulnerable to criticism. She was also able to acknowledge for the first time that she could now see that she had needed to keep the counsellor at arm's length for fear of experiencing the same feelings of envy and jealousy, and that was why she could not readily countenance interpretations about their relationship. By the end of the last session Ms H remained apprehensive about the future, but at the same time was able to take comfort in her sense of real achievement in the work, which she thought might be sufficient for the future.

In this example the counsellor could only engage tangentially with the client's main anxiety about the ending, how would she be able to internalize a good object, via an exploration of the security of her relationship with her boyfriend. Only when this was sufficiently worked through was Ms H able to give her attention to the ending of the counselling by reviewing the work as a whole. This process of *review* is an important part of the ending, as it helps the client put the work into perspective. Ms H could take pride in the achievements of the work, notably a growing conviction that misunderstandings and conflicts in relationships could be weathered. At the same time, she was able to voice some regrets about what was not done, in particular her acknowledgement of her need to keep the counsellor at a safe distance, which she realized had probably forestalled a closer exploration of her constant sense of disappointment in relationships. In this way Ms H got a bit closer to what was inevitably unfinished in the counselling, and to a greater appreciation of the loss of a productive and important relationship.

The end phase of the counselling is the last chance for any *unfinished business* in the counselling to be addressed. This grappling with incompleteness often makes the end phase feel messy and confusing. It also means that the predominant mood in this phase of the work is often a sense of satisfaction at good work done, but heavily marked by regret and disappointment at opportunities missed in the finite time available.

On time-limited, long-term and short-term work in counselling

Throughout this book, and especially in this last section, we have assumed that the ending date has already been agreed by counsellor and client at the start of the counselling, in other words that the work is time-limited, as this is almost always the case in public sector counselling and therapy organizations whose limited resources can rarely match the demand for their services. By contrast in private practice endings are usually open-ended, the actual termination date arrived at by negotiation between counsellor and client. This process of negotiation of the ending date with the counsellor can be a very fruitful experience for the client, reinforcing the truly co-operative dimension of the counselling work. But the intense anxieties brought about by the ending of the counselling are not usually lessened by having an open-ended contract, so that even when there is negotiation around the termination date, it can still not feel like there is sufficient time for the client to end well.

In time-limited work the ideal of a proper ending made when the client is ready can seem even more remote, as the client's sense of deprivation and emotional impoverishment can be powerfully accentuated by the fixing in advance of the termination date. So it sometimes happens, as the work nears its pre-determined end, that the client will indicate or directly ask for more time to be better prepared for the ending. The counsellor can feel under enormous pressure from the client to grant this reprieve from what can feel like the death sentence of an ending date that has come to represent the brutal cutting short of the work in progress. This pressure can be intensified by a sense that 'proper' psychoanalytic work means long-term work, and that therefore the counsellor is short-changing the client by giving them anything less.

The rationale for giving the client a longer rather than shorter period of counselling is that new developments, insights and states of mind need to become consolidated. This process, which is called *working-through* (see p. 19) can be compared to how we normally come to master a craft or skill. In his book *The Craftsman* the sociologist Richard Sennett makes the point that 'going over an action again and again ... enables self-criticism'. What is important for children in education, he writes, is 'the experience of studying their own ingrained practice and modulating it from within' (2008, pp. 37–8). We have seen this process of clients learning how to modulate their own practice from within in the examples of Ms H and Ms I in this chapter as they gradually over time became better at recognizing patterns in their own behaviour and experience. Their increased capacity for self-understanding came about by going over the same feelings, thoughts and events again and again. We tend to associate repetition with boredom, but this is to miss the connection between repetition and creativity:

> As skill expands, the capacity to sustain repetition increases. In music this is the so-called Isaac Stern rule, the great violinist declaring that the better your technique, the longer you can rehearse without becoming bored. (Sennett, 2008, p. 38)

But how long is 'sufficient time' or 'long enough' for a client? One way of trying to determine how long it takes for a client to master this process of self-modulation is to think in terms of the time needed to complete an experience. This was the way Winnicott thought of his work, modelled on his consultations with young children or babies and their mother. In these consultations he would place a shiny metal spatula on a table in front of the child, and wait and see what happens. Normally, after a period of hesitation, the child would reach for the spatula and then energetically bang on the table with it, or play with it in other ways. Often a game would ensue of throwing the spatula away, only for it to be retrieved by mother, until finally the child had had enough. Winnicott found that if any phase of this process was interrupted – for example by not allowing the child an initial period of hesitation in order to get over his or her anxiety at being in a new situation, or not allowing the child sufficient time to become fed up with the game of throwing away and retrieval – then the child was not able to complete the whole experience, and thus arrive at the end point of pleasure and mastery (Winnicott, 1941).

If we apply this idea of 'completing an experience' to the counselling as a whole, it is likely that some clients, particularly those with whom the working alliance always seems precarious and fragile (see next chapter), will need a period of longer-term in order to manage the tasks of the different phases of the work, especially the end phase which is likely to stir up intense feelings of abandonment. In many agencies 'long-term' work in counselling or psychotherapy would be taken to mean work of more than one year. But trying to translate the terms 'long-term' and 'short-term' into actual periods of time risks being both arbitrary and artificial. This is because thinking in purely quantitative terms, necessary though this is, can never do justice to the actual quality of the work. Sometimes, as we have seen, a particular experience involving self-understanding can be completed in a very short time frame, as we saw in the two assessment sessions with Mr G earlier in this chapter. Sometimes, even after a lengthy period, two years in the case of Ms J, more time was needed for the client to arrive at a more satisfactory ending to the work. Can one say that if the assessing counsellor with Mr G had given himself only one instead of two sessions, they would not have had the time to arrive at a satisfactory conclusion? Or if Ms J's counsellor had worked in a different way, or if Ms J had been seen by a different counsellor, the difficulties around ending the work would not have been so severe? Trying to answer these questions reveals the enormous complexity involved in trying think about the experience of time in psychodynamic work. It depends on the type of problem presented by the client, the time needed by the client to form a working alliance and to consolidate experiences, together with the counsellor's own pace of working, combined to form the unique counselling relationship established between the particular client and counsellor. This is why it is so hard with each client to predict at the outset how much time the client will need, and to judge as the ending approaches whether there is enough time for the client to come to a good enough conclusion of the work.

But despite this unpredictability counsellors still need to exercise their judgement. In the work with Ms H, for instance, difficult though the ending was, there was no indication that extending the ending date would have been of help to her (indeed, one might guess that if an extension to the ending date were given, all that would happen would be that another crisis with the boyfriend would then ensue). In the case of Ms J it did become clear that the client was ill-prepared to end the counselling, as she was still clinging on to an idealized transference. But this had to be accepted as part of the unfinished business of counselling. As with Ms H, there was no case to be made for postponing the date of termination. Rather than address the client's fears about the ending, such a policy would be more likely to reinforce her anxiety, as it would only confirm the client's underlying conviction that the ending of the counselling was indeed too awful to face. This is why it is rarely good practice to change an already agreed termination date. Nevertheless counsellors also need to be flexible if the situation so demands. For instance if by the end of the second assessment session Mr G had not been able to move on from his *impasse* with the counsellor, this would have been a good clinical reason for offering him a further session in order to try to bring the assessment to a satisfactory conclusion.

In order to be in the best position to make these judgements about time, it is helpful if the counsellor has experience of both long- and short-term work. Working with clients over a longer period (of at least six months, and preferably more than one year) can enable the counsellor to see for himself how the work can establish a momentum and reach a depth and intensity which is not possible over a shorter time. Furthermore over a longer period the counsellor can gain a clearer sense of the different phases of the work, particularly the middle phase with its emphasis on consolidation and the development of the transference which can get truncated in shorter time-frames. Experience in long-term work also helps the counsellor gain a sense of what can realistically be achieved in short-term work. But working without the luxury of more time can also be of value. In shorter-term work the counsellor has to learn to make interpretations when his understanding of the client is provisional and partial, and needs to make decisions about how to manage the transference when he knows less about the client and her emotional resources than he would like. Learning to think and to act under the pressure of a brief time-time can bring a quality of presence and directness to the counsellor's approach which can enrich his work with clients over longer periods. In short the counsellor can learn to help the client make the most of whatever time is available.

Summary

It can be helpful to think of the work with a client in terms of its different phases, each with its characteristic themes and challenges. Before the counsellor first meets the client at the start of the counselling, the client will have had an experience of the agency or organization in which the counsellor works. How the initial *referral* was managed, and how the entry into the organization through the *assessment* process was negotiated, will constitute some of what the client brings to the first session.

This initial engagement with the organization as a whole will either help or hinder the main task of the counsellor at the *beginning* phase of the work, which is to work towards the establishment of a working alliance with the client, so that the ground for the collaborative work that counselling entails can be laid. The solidity of the working alliance with the client is likely to be tested in the *middle* phase of the work, in which the client's characteristic defences are likely to fall under more intense scrutiny, which may precipitate a crisis in the work. If this crisis, in whatever form it takes, can be weathered sufficiently by both client and counsellor the working alliance will emerge further strengthened. The *end* phase of the work is likely to represent a further crisis in the work, as the client (and counsellor) may fear that whatever has been gained over the course of the work is likely to be lost once the counselling comes to an end. The more the client is able to acknowledge disappointment and regret at what has not been achieved in the counselling, alongside satisfaction and even pride in what has been gained, the more likely it is that the client can leave with a realistic sense of hope for the future. Consideration of how endings are managed in counselling leads on to a discussion of the differences between both short- and long-term work in counselling, and the value of each.

Further reading

Coren, A (2001) *Short-term Psychotherapy*, London: Palgrave.
Gray, A (1994) *An Introduction to the Therapeutic Frame,* London: Routledge.
Jacobs, M (1988) *Psychodynamic Counselling in Action,* London: Sage.
Murdin, L (1999) *How Much is Enough? Endings in Psychotherapy and Counselling,* London: Routledge.
Murdin, L and Errington, M (2005) *Setting Out: the importance of Beginnings in Psychotherapy and Counselling,* London: Brunner-Routledge.

8

WORKING WITH MORE DISTURBED CLIENTS

There have been a number of references so far in this book to clients who are clearly more disturbed in the sense that their functioning in the everyday world is impaired (e.g. Ronald Britton's patient in Chapter 1 who would try obsessively to flush her 'bad' thoughts down the toilet) or who are clearly psychiatrically ill (Rosenfeld's schizophrenic patient in Chapter 6). The theoretical chapters have given us the conceptual tools in order to understand such clients, in particular a description of the paranoid-schizoid position. We can now, in this chapter, present a more coherent picture of this mode of experience and the particular demands working with such clients make on the counsellor.

A therapeutic consultation with an ill child

In Chapter 1 we looked at a therapeutic consultation by Winnicott as an illustration of the nature of a therapeutic dialogue. In this consultation, Winnicott described several instances of how the boy he called Robin was able to make productive use of the sessions; notably in his ability and willingness to engage and become dependent in the limited way available in the session. For instance, Winnicott commented on Robin's capacity to be surprised by what he drew and on the sense of humour evident in his drawings, both of which he described as evidence of relative health, and therefore a resource for the therapist.

> A sense of humour is the ally of the therapist, who gets from it a feeling of confidence and a sense of having elbow-room for manoeuvring. It is evidence of the child's creative imagination and of happiness. (Winnicott, 1971, p. 32)

We can contrast this consultation with Robin with another of Winnicott's therapeutic consultations, this time with a boy called George where this capacity for engagement, and the consequent elbow room in the therapy was absent. George was 13, and had been brought to see Winnicott because he had been stealing and his behaviour was becoming delinquent. His behavioural problems had led to his being placed in a special school, but this place was now in jeopardy as a result of his recent behaviour.

In the consultation George was able to take part in the Squiggle Game, Winnicott's way of using drawings in order to make contact with a child (see Chapter 1, p. 14). However Winnicott was quickly struck by two features of George's drawings. Some of the drawings themselves were of isolated parts of the body (e.g. a man's head, a hand, a crab's claw) and there were no drawings which incorporated a whole body or of people being together. George also did a number of other drawings, or elaborated Winnicott's squiggles, into rather strange shapes or lines, to which he gave titles such as 'a thing from outer space', 'a shadow moving fast' or 'a nothing'. The impression Winnicott gained from his drawings, and his elaborations of Winnicott's drawings was that George's inner world consisted of bits of objects, which had no relation to each other, and of strange and meaningless events.

Winnicott further noted that George did not find any of his weird drawings funny. Indeed not only was there no evidence of a sense of humour or surprise, which might have suggested some creativity, but Winnicott found it hard to know what George might be feeling or thinking about his drawings at all, or indeed about the consultation as a whole. 'I was employing a technique with a boy who looked nice and was nicely dressed and who had good manners and yet who seemed to be in some strange way absent' (1971, p. 384).

There were, however, a few occasions when George was able to show something more than compliance. After a conversation about playing football, George elaborated one of Winnicott's drawings in what Winnicott described as 'a surprisingly rich way', by turning it into a rather weird and ugly head, but drawn with more feeling and engagement than his earlier strange drawings. Then George made a drawing himself of what he called a shadow moving fast, and showed Winnicott where the eyes, nose and mouth could be seen. He then elaborated a drawing of Winnicott's into a strange kind of elongated figure which he called 'a nothing'. Winnicott felt that with these drawings George had loosened up as far as he was able and was now communicating something of himself, that at the core of himself he felt there was nothing.

With no sense of a solid or coherent core, parts of the self could not be linked together, but co-existed in isolation from each other. So, for example, George had been stealing from his mother from the age of four, and often told her that he didn't want to steal from her and that he couldn't help it. But while telling her this he still went on stealing from her, as though his wish could not connect up with his action. He showed no evidence of a desire to understand why this might be so. He had little or no capacity to be curious or thoughtful about himself or the world. 'The question as to whether he was glad to be a boy or whether he would ever have liked to be a girl meant nothing to him, as could be predicted. He took himself entirely for granted, built as he was on conformity' (Winnicott, 1971, p. 384).

Unlike the boy called Robin, who was able to engage with Winnicott in such a way as to make use of the consultation and find helpful some of the things said to him, the rigidity of George's defences allowed him little space to receive anything of value. Even so, there was a development after the consultation, reported to Winnicott by the mother, which showed some movement.

> After my interview with this boy he said to his mother: 'It's funny, the doctor asked me if I ever dreamed about stealing or burglars and I told him that I have never dreamed that kind of dream. But after I saw him I had a dream in which I had stolen a wallet and I went off to the next town where I stole another wallet and then I had to go to another town where I stole another wallet, and so it went on. It's funny, I have never dreamed about stealing before.' (1971, p. 380)

For Winnicott, this was a sign that George, through his dreaming, was trying to get in touch with a dissociated part of himself which lay behind his need to steal. This would then need to be the focus if any therapeutic work was to be done with George, to try to reach this split-off part which was expressing itself through compulsive stealing, and see where it came from (e.g. was it an attempt to make up for some early and profound sense of emotional deprivation?).

The most striking feature of this boy's experience was its degree of *dissociation,* as though he consisted of different selves, or parts of his ego, which had lives independent of each other. This quality also comes over in the fragmentation of his experience. The most powerful way this impacted on Winnicott was in the sense of *absence*. Winnicott felt he was in the presence of a shell, someone who was compliant but unreal in some profound and disturbing way. In terms of his conduct of the consultation, these two qualities of dissociation and absence translated into a thin and precarious working alliance, that is a sense of cooperative working which was limited and superficial. Any therapeutic help offered would have to work with this limitation.

We can use these criteria – the dissociation, fragmentation or splitting (these terms overlap) of experience, the quality of absence or emptiness behind a superficial or false front, and the thinness of the working alliance – to identify the main features of clients whom we can call more disturbed, in the sense that their experience is predominantly in the paranoid-schizoid mode. In the psychoanalytic literature (which here draws on the diagnostic categories of psychiatry) neurotic experience and behaviour which designates what one might call the normal difficulties in living of the depressive position (such as shown by Mrs A) are distinguished from two other states of mind which characterize more disturbed experience and behaviour. These are psychosis on the one hand and borderline or narcissistic states on the other.

Psychosis

We all know in a rough and ready way what psychosis is, that it entails a massive withdrawal from the world of everyday reality and its replacement by another kind of imaginary world which obeys magical laws. In this world the psychotic person might hear voices that aren't there (auditory hallucinations), see things that don't exist (visual hallucinations) or believe things that are not true (delusions). The psychoanalytic understanding of psychosis is to construe it as a massive and desperate response to a perceived threat of the total annihilation of the mind. Whether this threat is a real one, for example manifested by the conscious or unconscious hatred or murderousness of the parental figures, or whether it is more of a response to persistent and massive experiences of uncontainment, the result is that the persecution is introjected, so that the person experiences the deadly attack as coming from his own internal bad objects. Rather like the fox, which bites off his own leg in order to free himself from a trap, the mind in its psychotic frenzy then seeks to destroy part of itself in order to escape from this internal threat. In psychosis the part that is attacked is the mind's ability to apprehend external reality, its perceptual and thinking apparatus.

In order to try to understand such a process the psychoanalyst Edna O'Shaughnessy invites us to imagine the following scenario. Normally, she says, an infant who feels frustration, for instance hunger, will be able to translate his awareness of his hunger into some action which will bring his hunger to an end, for example crying for his mother. But an infant who can tolerate little or no frustration, as it brings terrifying anxieties of annihilation (e.g. frustration may be experienced as an internal attack by the infant's bad objects) will be driven to extreme and even bizarre measures in an attempt to get rid of his awareness of frustration in the first place.

> I have in mind an infant who lay in his pram in the garden from eight o'clock in the morning to late afternoon, not crying but gazing at the leaves of the trees.... Instead of beginning to develop a mind for thinking, it is likely that such a psyche has become an apparatus for ridding itself of bad objects. It does this by the minute fragmentation and projection of incipient thoughts, sensations, and also the sense organs which threaten to bring awareness of internal or external reality. The infant in my example perhaps used his eyes as channels for projecting the unwanted fragments of his personality into external objects. On this model we can understand how the infant under the trees is free of hunger and terror because his psyche is in fragments in the leaves. (O'Shaughnessy, 1992, p. 91)

So O'Shaughnessy invites us to imagine a projection so massive that there is scarcely any sense of self or ego left, or what is left has little strength or coherence to provide any real sense of identity or coherence. Such an infant as he grows up will, for some or most of the time be seriously and profoundly confused about his own aliveness and whether objects and people in his own life have any independent existence of their own. O'Shaughnessy draws on the work of Wilfred Bion (who did most to elaborate this particular way of thinking about psychosis), who said of the psychotic that 'he moves, not in a world of dreams, but in a world of objects which are ordinarily the furniture of dreams' (Symington and Symington, 1996, p. 93).

Counsellors may not ordinarily come across many clients who are manifestly psychotic or psychiatrically ill, and if they did would probably refer them on to the psychiatric services or specialist counselling or psychotherapy agencies, feeling they would be out of their depth in working with such severe illness. But such clients can be given something of value by counsellors who have the necessary training and experience, and also the resilience and imagination in order to deal with the manifestly psychotic anxieties and defences with which they will be faced (Nicholas, 1992) as in the following example.

Mr K was a man in his late forties who had spent over fifteen years of his life in a psychiatric hospital, with a diagnosis of chronic schizophrenia. He now lived alone in the community. His sister, with whom Mr K had spor-adic contact, had requested counselling help for him from a local counsel-ling centre which offered supportive counselling for mentally ill clients. The (male) counsellor who took on the case wrote to Mr K to see if he wanted counselling, and Mr K wrote back, saying he did, but that he was too fright-ened to leave his house, and so could he be visited at home. The agency had a commitment to reaching out to very ill clients, and so encouraged its workers to visit clients at home if they were unable to come to the counsel-ling centre. The counsellor therefore, wrote back agreeing to meet Mr K at his home and giving the time of his appointment.

The counsellor called at the appointed time and rang the bell repeatedly. Eventually the door opened, and he was let in by Mr K, who showed him to a sparsely furnished and rather shabby sitting room. Mr K sat down, and the counsellor realized there were no other chairs in the room. In fact the room was full of cardboard boxes and piles of newspapers arranged around the perimeter, with Mr K's chair and a table in the centre. The counsellor asked if he could sit on one of the cardboard boxes, and Mr K said yes.

The counsellor then introduced himself and asked Mr K if he could say more about why he had asked for counselling help. Mr K spoke haltingly but intelligibly about being glad to have been discharged from psychiatric hos-pital, but also missing some of the patients and staff he had known, and not knowing what to do about it. He asked the counsellor whether he thought he could help him with this, and the counsellor said he was willing to give it a go. There was then a long and awkward silence. The counsellor asked about Mr K's time in hospital, and about his family and whether he had any kind of social life. Mr K replied in factual terms only, telling the counsel-lor how long he had been in hospital, the names of the some of the people he had known, how many brothers and sisters he had and that his parents were both dead, and that he had two male friends who had also been dis-charged from the hospital. The counsellor was quite unable to elicit any feel-ings about any of this information. The session continued in this manner, with the counsellor asking a few questions about Mr K's life and getting short, factual answers. At the end of the session the counsellor said that he was able to come and visit Mr K once a week, at a regular time for up to a year. Mr K said that would be fine. He got up from his chair and showed the counsellor out.

At the time of his next session Mr K did not answer the door (the counsellor was as sure as he could be that he was in the house), and the counsellor had to leave without seeing Mr K. He wrote to say he was sorry Mr K had not felt able to let him in, and that, unless he heard otherwise, he would come at the agreed time next week. After that Mr K was always there to open the door, except after a holiday break in the counselling, when the door remained firmly closed at the session which followed the gap.

In the second session the conversation again remained almost exclusively on the factual and concrete level. Mr K would tell the counsellor of incidents in his daily life, and share some memories about his time in hospital. These were told with little evident feeling, as though they had happened to someone else. He became most animated when talking about cars, about which he had a great knowledge and interest. He had worked as an apprentice mechanic in a garage before he became ill and was admitted to hospital, and would talk at some length about the different kinds of cars he had worked on, what kind of engine each car had, how the body was put together and so on. Initially the counsellor found this topic of conversation very boring, but in time he came to see that this was Mr K's way of talking about aspects of himself. It was as though Mr K only felt safe enough to come alive if he assumed the identity of a solid thing.

Being safe was of paramount importance to Mr K. He rarely left his house for fear of being mugged. In fact he rarely left the sitting room, as he sometimes felt the other rooms in the house not to be safe. On one occasion when the counsellor was let in for a session Mr K hovered in the hall, saying he could no longer get into the sitting room, and the counsellor could see boxes and piles of newspapers spilling out of the door. This was the occasion when Mr K felt most psychotic, spending the session pacing up and down the hall with a terrified look on his face, and talking to himself in an agitated and confused manner.

Over time the counsellor learnt to see the state of the sitting room as the best indicator of Mr K's state of mind. If the cardboard boxes and piles of newspapers were pushed back against the walls, giving a sense of space in the centre of the room where he and Mr K sat, the counsellor could look forward to Mr K being more talkative and open to making contact in his limited way. If however, the boxes and newspapers were encroaching on the space in the middle, as though threatening to take over the room, then the counsellor would either find Mr K in an uncommunicative mood, sometimes literally saying nothing for a whole session, or in a paranoid state, speaking of how frightening it was to live in the world. For the counsellor the state of the living room came to be an indicator of whether there was a 'non-psychotic' part of Mr K's mind with which he could make contact (the space in the middle of the room), or whether this 'non-psychotic' part had been taken over by the psychotic parts of Mr K's personality.

With so little of the normal supports to rely on, the counsellor paid special attention to his counter-transference reactions in order to help him make sense of Mr K's experience and behaviour. He used his own experience of never knowing whether he would be let in to the house by Mr K to speak to him about the uncertainty and unpredictability of the world he inhabited. Drawing on how unwelcome he was made to feel, the counsellor spoke of how Mr K felt like an unwelcome stranger in the world. When he sat in the middle of the sitting-room, hemmed in by the invading cardboard boxes and newspapers he talked to Mr K about how he could not deal with the rubbish in his head, and feared being taken over by the bad or menacing parts of his own mind. Such interpretations seemed to calm Mr K (and certainly helped the counsellor survive the bizarreness of the situation he found himself in), as though some order and meaning could be found in the surrounding madness.

After several months Mr K was sometimes able to speak of one or two of the people he had known in hospital as though they meant something to him and it mattered that he no longer had any dealings with them. He started to imagine what they might be doing with their lives since he had last had contact with them. On such occasions the counsellor was filled with an overwhelming and almost unbearable sense of sadness, a feeling which lasted for several days after his visit. Towards the end of the counselling Mr K was able to tell the counsellor that he did now have some understanding of what it was like to miss someone, and he thanked the counsellor for having helped him.

However the ending of the counselling was clearly too painful for Mr K to bear, and for the final three sessions the counsellor was never let into the house. He wrote to Mr K to acknowledge the end of the counselling, and received a brief note thanking him for his time, but also saying he did not wish to be visited again by any more counsellors.

As this example shows, much of the work with a psychotic client is in managing one's own counter-transference. The counsellor had to deal with his own massive feelings of rejection, of feeling useless, of boredom in the face of Mr K's frequent silences or apparent irrelevancies, of bewilderment at the strangeness of Mr K's behaviour and surroundings. Only when he no longer felt overwhelmed or too disturbed by such feelings was he then freed up to use his theoretical knowledge and his own counter-transference reactions to make some sense of Mr K's experience and put this across to him in words. This offered sufficient containment for Mr K to acknowledge near the end of the counselling that he now finally understood what it meant to miss someone. This may well have been the first time Mr K had ever experienced feelings of sadness or loss without an accompanying terror of going mad, and would very likely have been his first experience of being in the presence of a containing person. So even though there were no outward signs of improvement in Mr K's life – and indeed Mr K indicated that he did not wish the experience of counselling to be repeated, perhaps because he had found the experience of missing his friends to be very painful – the counselling must have been of incalculable benefit to him.

Narcissistic and borderline states of mind

Unless he is working in a specialist setting which deals with the mentally ill, the counsellor may well not come across such a manifestly ill patient as Mr K in his normal counselling work. However, there is a range of clients who are not psychotic in the sense of being out of touch with reality and unable to function in the world, but whose sense of integrity and continuity is at times so precarious that they frequently have to make use of psychotic defences. Such clients, whose experience is predominantly in the paranoid-schizoid mode but who might be capable at times, to move towards the depressive position, can be encountered in any counselling setting. In the clinical literature they are usually referred to as manifesting a narcissistic or borderline personality or state.

Freud used the term narcissism to designate a form of psychic functioning in which the ego turns its back on the external world and relationships with others, instead taking itself as the object of its interest and love. The narcissistic person, in his hatred of the frustrations of reality, refuses to give up or returns to the omnipotence of the infant or child, who regards himself as the centre of the universe. Such a person will often come over as arrogant or bombastic, but this hard exterior is designed to protect an ego which actually feels extremely vulnerable and fragile (see, for example, Mr C in Chapter 5). The hard outer shell gives a form of stability and consistency to his experience, but this rigid structure is really hollow and, if threatened, the narcissistic person will feel at risk of catastrophic collapse.

The terms 'borderline personality' or 'borderline state of mind', like the narcissistic state, describe a way of psychic functioning which lies between neurosis and psychosis. But the borderline lacks the apparent stability of the narcissist. The clinical picture tends towards chaotic and impulsive acting out, as in suicidal or self-hating episodes, as feelings, thoughts and impulses are typically experienced as overwhelming and uncontrollable (see, for example, Ms B in Chapter 4 and Ms F in Chapter 5, both of whom display borderline features).

When it comes to relationships with others, the narcissistic person is likely to be capable only of making superficial relationships, or, where he is able to become dependent, to deny his need and project it into the other person, whom he therefore treats as being dependent on him. The borderline person will tend to oscillate violently between either feeling overwhelmed by and intruded upon by the other, or utterly ignored and rejected. Neither can find a satisfactory position in relationships, one which is neither totally dependent nor utterly independent, not too close and not too distant.

The dissociation and fragmentation of experience, together with the absence of a solid and coherent sense of self, is not as massive or global as in psychosis. The person in a narcissistic or borderline state may well be capable of making relationships and living an ordinary life in the world. However this ability to live an ordinary life in the world will typically feel precarious and in danger of imminent collapse.

This makes the establishment of a positive transference, and thus a working alliance problematic in work with more disturbed clients. With the more neurotic client (such as Mrs A) a sense of mutuality about the aims and value of the counselling can develop. The counsellor can rely on the work being a shared enterprise when the going gets tough. The ability of the client to cooperate in the work means that acting out by the client is likely to be limited and recoverable. But all of this presupposes the client's ability to negotiate the degree of involvement with the counsellor, to be affected without feeling taken over or invaded, or to feel separate without feeling abandoned and discarded. With clients functioning at a borderline or narcissistic level none of this can be assumed. What might look like cooperative working together is more likely to be compliance on the part of the client, who feels he or she has to submit to the demands of the counsellor in order not to be abandoned. Where more genuine contact is made, this is likely to provoke fear and hatred in the client, fear of the counsellor getting inside and taking over and hatred of the counsellor for being separate and not available all the time.

The upshot of all this is that counsellors working with more disturbed clients must be prepared to encounter not only more demanding or challenging behaviour from their clients, but also more extreme or disturbing reactions to the counselling itself. More disturbed clients are more likely to act out, that is resort to self-destructive, destructive or delinquent behaviour during counselling. They will be more prone to powerful and primitive transference relationships with the counsellor, thereby provoking more disturbing counter-transference reactions on the counsellor's part. And fear of breakdown and madness is much more likely to be in evidence. These features are illustrated in the following example.

Mr L was a lonely and isolated middle-aged single man, who had suffered on and off from depression since early adolescence. His depression was sometimes accompanied by suicidal thoughts, and he had on one occasion made a serious suicide attempt. He sought help after he had recently been made redundant from his job as a postman, which had brought about a return of his depression with particular severity. In the past his depression had been treated by drugs, but now he wanted to try counselling. He was referred by his psychiatrist to a local counselling agency which specialized in working with mental illness, and was seen by a male counsellor, who offered him weekly sessions of up to two years. In view of the fact that Mr L had made a serious suicide attempt in the past, the counsellor made it a condition of the counselling that Mr L would continue to see the psychiatrist at regular intervals. The counsellor felt it necessary to establish this supportive network from the outset, reasoning that if the counselling was going to get anywhere, it was likely to stir up similar anxieties and terrors which had led Mr L to try to kill himself in the past. Mr L was happy to agree to these conditions, indeed saying that they made him feel safer about starting counselling.

Mr L used the early sessions to talk reflectively about his relationship with his parents. This quickly led him to start to re-evaluate how he saw them as he found himself forced to recognize the emotional and, at least on one occasion, sexual abuse he had suffered at their hands. From having thought of his parents as flawed but basically good, he was now having to think of them as seriously negligent if not malevolent. Six weeks after starting counselling he came to his session and told the counsellor that two days previously he had taken a serious overdose. To his disappointment he had not died, and on waking up had gone to the hospital and had his stomach pumped out.

Mr L told the counsellor that he had tried to kill himself because he saw counselling as his last chance of finding some meaning and hope in his life, yet it had only made his pain worse. Instead of strengthening him, counselling was making him weaker. Although what he had said about his parents were things he had always known, and it was a relief to be able to share these feelings and thoughts about them, he now felt that his ideal images of them had been taken away and he was left with nothing.

Nevertheless, despite the pain it was causing him, Mr L said he wanted to carry on with the counselling. His attempt to kill himself had brought home to him how self-destructive he was, and he wanted to understand this part of himself better. His psychiatrist, whom Mr L had agreed with the counsellor to consult after the suicide attempt, supported his wish to continue in counselling. This gave the counsellor confidence that he could rely on a containing professional network if Mr L became suicidal in the counselling again.

It soon became clear that Mr L's rage and hatred were initially directed towards other people and only subsequently turned round against himself. For instance he told many stories of people getting in his way or pushing him about in the street and how he was left boiling inside with impotent rage. He played the part of the dutiful son to his parents, but underneath felt furious with them for not really caring about him. The counsellor attempted to bring this rage into the transference by pointing out how angry Mr L was with him, for example, for having taken away his idealized images of his parents. The counsellor also interpreted Mr L's suicide attempt as motivated by rage, against his parents for their neglect and abuse, and against himself for not only having failed to help him in counselling but also for having caused him more pain. Mr L responded to such interpretations by compliantly agreeing with their logic, saying they 'made sense intellectually to him'. He could acknowledge being angry with his parents for what they had done to him in the past, but could see no point in continuing to feel angry and now felt nothing towards them, and he denied feeling any rage or hatred towards the counsellor.

In the face of this blanket denial, little progress could be made in helping Mr L become more in touch with his feelings. But what could be explored were Mr L's characteristic defences against feeling, particularly those which manifested themselves directly in the counselling. For example, from time to time Mr L would go blank in a session, that is switch off from what the counsellor was saying. These periods of blankness would normally last only a few minutes, after which Mr L would have to ask the counsellor to repeat what he had just said. The counsellor gained some insight into the meaning of these dissociated states by exploring his own counter-transference reaction to Mr L's dissociation from his feelings, which was on occasions to feel overwhelmed with drowsiness, so much so that he could barely keep his eyes open. He was able to think of these narcoleptic states as a struggle between a part of him which wanted to keep in contact with Mr L and another part of him which could not bear this closeness and wanted to kill it off. This helped him

understand Mr L's own desperate struggle between life and death. The
counsellor linked Mr L's blank states directly to his self-destructiveness
by describing them to Mr L as mini-suicide attempts, in which he killed
off any contact with the counsellor. These interpretations did make some
impact on Mr L, as they showed his self-destructiveness to be an active
and potent force in the counselling itself.

By the end of the counselling Mr L did feel his pull towards self-
destructiveness was less powerful, and more a part of himself which he could
try to accept. He felt he had gained in confidence sufficiently to apply to
train for a new job, and also felt more able to socialize with others and make
friends. Characteristically, however, he left the counselling on a despairing
and self-destructive note, saying counselling had failed and that he still saw
his life as pointless and empty. (Spurling, 2003, pp. 25–41)

The case of Mr L illustrates some of the difficulties in working with
more disturbed clients. The pull towards acting out can be very
strong, and can have a powerfully inhibiting effect on the counselling. Mr L's suicide attempt early in the counselling cast a long
shadow over the rest of the work as a terrible demonstration of what
he might resort to if he found the counselling too painful. Mr L
remained stuck in the paranoid-schizoid position, feeling constantly
at risk of attack from other people, and from his own persecutory
internal objects. With an absence of any good or sustaining figures
in Mr L's background who could form the basis for a strong positive transference, he did not feel safe enough in the counselling to
explore his negative transference in any depth. Instead he defended
himself from both external and internal attack by keeping his hostile feelings as far apart from his loving feelings as possible, for fear
that the bad would contaminate the good, and then projecting his
hostility and rage into other people so as to be rid of such feelings.
But such massive splitting and projection left him feeling hollow,
with no depth to his feelings. Mr L could not tolerate any feelings
associated with the depressive position – loss, sadness, concern or
guilt – as these only left him feeling even more empty and bereft.
Hence his blank states during the counselling, which killed off any
feelings of contact with or dependence on the counsellor, and also
his attack on the value of the counselling at the end, in order to avoid
feelings of loss.

The counsellor working with more disturbed clients will have
to contain the very powerful and often disturbing nature of the
projections put into him, which are likely to threaten his belief
in himself as an effective or helpful figure. A crucial part of the

counsellor's work with Mr L involved tolerating the deathly narcoleptic states to which he was subjected, and more generally
managing his own counter-transference reactions to Mr L of feeling either passively useless or actively cruel in subjecting him to
further pain.

In view of the risk of breakdown, the danger of acting out and
the strain put on the counsellor's ability to function as a counsellor, working with more disturbed clients may be better done,
and indeed may require a wider, containing environment within
which the work with the client can be located. This may mean the
counsellor working in an institutional setting or within a professional network. Although Mr K had little formal contact with the
counselling agency where his counsellor worked, he did have a
good relationship with his sister who made the initial referral,
and this helped him see the counselling agency as a safe place and
enabled him to sustain a belief in the counsellor as a reliable person. Mr L had confidence in the referring psychiatrist, who also
saw him after his suicide attempt, and he experienced the professional link between the counsellor and psychiatrist as supportive.
With both clients their positive transference to the wider network
was an important factor in their finding some containment in the
counselling.

Summary

In this chapter we have looked at the diagnostic distinctions
between neurotic, psychotic and borderline or narcissistic states of
mind. Diagnosis is important as it determines the way the counsellor approaches his work with clients. In psychoanalytic thinking
'neurotic' is linked with experiences in the depressive mode, and
with 'normal', in the sense that whatever difficulties or symptoms
are being presented, the neurotic client takes for granted, at least for
much of the time, a more-or-less stable sense of self and coherence
of experience. In clinical work the counsellor can aim to establish a
working alliance with the neurotic client which will sustain both
parties through the inevitable periods of turbulence in the counselling relationship.

By contrast, psychotic clients have little sense of having a self or
of experience being coherent. Their inner world is made up of bits
of objects which are experienced as both meaningless and dangerous. Faced with experiences which threaten to overwhelm and
annihilate them, the psychotic person has recourse to violent and

primitive methods of defence, notably the fragmenting of experience (so that bad experiences do not contaminate good ones) and the projection of frightening or dangerous parts of oneself into other people or into objects in the physical world. The primary task for the counsellor who encounters such manifestly ill clients will be to manage, and not be overwhelmed by his own anxiety in the face of the madness and bizarre behaviour of the psychotic client.

There are also clients who can function in the world in the way a neurotic can, but whose experience is predominantly in the paranoid-schizoid mode, and whose sense of themselves as coherent or stable is much more precarious. Such people, called borderline or narcissistic in the psychoanalytic literature, will rely on the more primitive defences employed by the psychotic in order to hold themselves together. Whereas the practicing counsellor is not very likely to encounter manifestly psychotic clients, those who are more disturbed in the sense of being borderline or narcissistic are frequent users of counselling services and the counsellor needs to have some idea of what to expect in working with them. More disturbed clients are more likely to resort to acting out, often in destructive or self-destructive ways. As there may well be no good figures in the client's past, a positive transference to the counsellor and the work will be much more difficult, and may not be achieved at all. The more disturbed client is likely to have difficulty in keeping hold of the symbolic or 'as if' quality of the transference, and the counsellor will have to manage powerful and disturbing counter-transference reactions to his client (although not as global or bizarre as in psychosis). In order to offer such clients an experience of containment the counsellor may need the support of an institutional setting or professional network.

Further reading

Arthur, A (2000) 'Psychodynamic counselling for the borderline personality disordered client: a case study', *Psychodynamic Counselling*, vol. 6, no. 1, pp. 31–48.

Malan, D (1979) 'Primitive phenomena', Ch. 15 of *Individual Psychotherapy and the Science of Psychodynamics*, London: Butterworths.

McLean, D and Nathan, J (2007) 'Treatment of Personality Disorder: Limit Setting and the Use of Benign Authority, *British Journal of Psychotherapy*, vol. 23, no. 2, pp. 231–46.

Noonan, E (1983) 'The framework: diagnosis', Ch. 3 of *Counselling Young People*, London: Methuen.

Spurling, L (2003) 'Transference with the borderline client: some implications for training psychodynamic counsellors', *Psychodynamic Practice*, vol. 9, no. 1, pp. 25–41.

Terry, P (2003) 'Working with psychosis: part one: grieving the damage of a psychotic illness', *Psychodynamic Practice*, vol. 9, no. 2, pp. 123–41.

Terry, P (2004) 'Working with psychosis: part 2 – encounters with the Omnipotent Super-Ego', *Psychodynamic Practice*, vol. 10, no. 1, pp. 45–59.

Terry, P (2005) 'Working with psychosis: part 3 – struggling to contain madness – losing and recovering a capacity to think', *Psychodynamic Practice*, vol. 11, no. 1, pp. 29–40.

9

THE ORGANIZATIONAL FRAMEWORK

In this book we have paid particular attention to the quality of the relationship between counsellor and client, seeing this focus as the hallmark of a psychodynamic approach. It can be tempting, therefore, to see anything that happens outside of this client-counsellor dyad as not part of the 'real' work of counselling; indeed to think of it as an interference with the work. But this is to forget that the counselling relationship occurs within a setting, and that part of this setting is constituted by the professional and organizational *context* within which the counselling takes place.

The professional context is present, for example, in the theory on which the counsellor draws and the technique which he employs, which link him to bodies of knowledge, skill and professional practice in the psychoanalytic and counselling worlds. This wider context is present even where the counselling seems to focus most on the client's relationship with the counsellor, that is in the transference relationship. As we have seen (p. 115), transference can be understood as the creation in the counselling of a third figure in the counselling relationship, one constructed by both client and counsellor. Another way of putting this is to think of the counsellor/client relationship not as essentially dyadic but as having a triangular or oedipal structure, in which the dyad always points beyond itself to a relationship with a third.

In an organizational setting this third figure, as well as having features of the client's internal world, is also bound to represent some features of the client's experience of the organization within which the counselling takes place. This might express itself in terms of an actual figure with whom the client feels involved, maybe another professional, administrator or receptionist with whom the client has built up a relationship. Or it may be another service within the organization, or the bricks-and-mortar building itself in which the organization is housed, which comes to serve an important function for the client, for example as representing a place which is familiar and feels safe. Some clients speak of having a long association with an organization, which they come to regard like a family. So there will always be a transference not only to the person of the counsellor but also to the organization in which the counsellor works, and this more impersonal form of transference to the counsellor as part of an organization may provide a vital holding function for some more disturbed clients (see Chapter 8).

As well as having a transference dimension, the organization will impinge on the counsellor's relationship with the client in more direct ways. The way the organization views its purpose, defines its particular philosophy, organizes the ways referrals and assessments are managed, determines the length of the counselling work, and so on – all of these will directly affect how the counsellor conducts himself in his work. Indeed the counsellor's very identity is constituted by the implicit assumptions and ideals as well as the more explicit expectations and prescriptions of the organization in which he works, for instance in the title or designation he is given in his organization and how this is understood.

An organizational perspective: understanding role, task, boundaries, culture and authority

In speaking of the counsellor's identity in its organizational dimension we are led to consider his *role* in that organization, that is how he understands what is expected of him and how he carries it out (see also p. 36). Managing himself in role inevitably involves the counsellor in thinking of his relationship with his colleagues, and to the organization as a whole.

> In order to manage oneself in role, the fundamental question is 'How far can I mobilize my resources and potential to contribute to the task?' This requires recognition of where one's role ends and another person's begins, the scope and limits of one's own authority, and a readiness to sanction that of others. (Obholzer & Roberts 1994, p. 44)

So to conceive of oneself in terms of role brings with it an idea of the tasks one has to perform. Each organization can be thought of as having a *primary task*, that is an idea about why it exists and what its purpose is. How an organization understands its primary task will affect, for example, how it manages referrals into the agency – does the organization believe it is there to accept all clients, whatever their problems, or does it consider itself to have a more specific brief as to which clients to accept, for example, only those who meet certain criteria? The primary task is related to what can be called the *culture* of a particular organization, that is its implicit beliefs and assumptions about its purpose and how that can be brought about. These ideas, held in common, lead to characteristic work practices, and also to the creation of a distinctive emotional atmosphere in any organization, 'the particular way we do things here'. For example, is there an idea that clients need to be actively engaged by promoting a mood and ambiance of informality, as sometimes happens in organizations offering counselling to young people? Or is there more of a sense of potential clients needing to be carefully assessed so that those deemed 'unsuitable' can be weeded out and sent elsewhere, as is more likely in the various departments in the National Health Service? The way each organization understands its primary task and culture will also affect the type of *boundaries* of the organization, that is what kinds of interchange it permits or encourages between its different parts, or between itself as a whole and the outside world. Likewise the nature of authority and *leadership* in each organization, for example, democratic or hierarchical, will vary depending on its understanding of its primary task and how this is to be brought about.

Making use of an organizational understanding: two examples

These conceptual tools are useful for the counsellor in thinking about the organizational framework in which he works. Often this framework will operate just below his level of awareness and will not be seen to directly impinge upon his work. But sometimes organizational dynamics are encountered head on as in the following examples.

The manager of a residential unit for psychiatric patients discharged from a mental hospital contacted a local counselling centre to ask whether she could refer some of the residents of the unit for counselling. The centre allocated one counsellor to work with clients from this unit. Three clients were referred from the unit, and work with all of them at the counselling centre started well. The clients were all keen to talk about their life in the mental hospital and what it had been like to leave. After a few sessions, however, the first client began to express doubts about whether he needed any more counselling. It then emerged from this client that he had talked about the counselling to his key worker at the unit, and this key worker had expressed some doubts about the value of 'raking up all your feelings about things in the past'. In the next session the client told the counsellor that he thought it better to 'let sleeping dogs lie' and that he had decided to end the counselling.

A similar pattern arose in the work with the other two clients. Both clients decided to end their counselling soon after the first client left.

The counsellor, disheartened and feeling that she had mismanaged the counselling by not making it safe enough for the clients to want to continue, reported what had happened to her colleagues at the counselling centre. The team were supportive, telling her that they could not see how she could have done more as a counsellor, and that they thought the problem lay not with her work with the clients but with the residential unit and its ambivalent attitude about its residents receiving counselling. They advised the counsellor to meet with the manager of the unit to discuss why all three clients had broken off their contact.

The counsellor duly met the manager and was told that the unit had been set up in the wake of the closure of the mental hospital which had housed the residents of the unit, and in fact some of the staff at the unit had also worked at the hospital. These staff tended to work in more traditional ways, relying on medical forms of intervention, and were suspicious of any kind of therapy or counselling. However she had also recruited some new staff members, who were interested not so much in 'maintaining' the residents but in actively 'changing' them, so that they might one day be capable of independent living. These staff members were strongly in favour of the residents receiving counselling. It became clear to the counsellor that the clients were caught in the middle of this conflict between the staff. The counsellor told the manager her view, and said that there was no chance of further counselling succeeding unless these mixed messages could be addressed.

The manager and counsellor agreed that the manager would raise this issue of the mixed messages about counselling with the staff, and see if there was a willingness to take the issue further. The manager subsequently contacted the counsellor to say that the staff were open to discussion about this, and asked whether the counsellor would be willing to attend a staff meeting at the unit to talk about what counselling was and how it might help the residents. The counsellor agreed to this, but feeling she needed to be seen by the staff as endorsed by the manager, she asked the manager to be present at this meeting as well.

At the staff meeting the counsellor presented her view of what had happened with the counselling. She said that the three clients who had been referred had begun by getting some benefit from counselling, but had then reported receiving mixed messages about the value of counselling from the staff. This had led them to feel confused and unsafe, and so each had decided to end the counselling prematurely. Although initially wary of speaking in front of the counsellor, the staff, encouraged by the manager, started to give their views about the value of counselling. This gradually led to the staff being able to speak quite openly about their feelings about the unit and about each other. The staff who had previously worked in the hospital said they thought they were seen by the new staff as old-fashioned and resistant to change. They felt their long experience of working with the residents in the hospital was neither recognized nor valued. The new staff said that they felt their ideas on trying to create a more therapeutic environment in the unit were dismissed by the old staff as fashionable and trendy. The old staff denied they were opposed to adopting a more therapeutic approach, but added that they sometimes felt that the new staff could not face the fact that many of the residents were too ill to be able to cope with a less structured environment.

The counsellor listened carefully to each ideological position, and by the end of the meeting both sets of staff felt they had been listened to and agreed to have further meetings with both manager and counsellor to see if they could work better together. Over the course of several more meetings the staff were able to openly acknowledge their different views, and begin to think about the value of the ideas of their colleagues who thought differently, even if they did not agree with them. Attention was also paid to the confusing effect on the residents of this important difference in the way the staff thought about their work.

As a result of this better working environment the staff, helped by the manager, worked out a coherent policy about residents seeking counselling. One particular staff member, in whom both 'camps' had confidence, was designated as the co-ordinator of counselling. He would decide, in consultation with both residents and staff whom to refer to counselling. This staff member would also liase with the counsellor on the progress of the counselling and keep the staff at the unit informed. This new system worked much better. The three clients initially referred returned for further counselling, and several new referrals were made. All of these clients were helped to stay in counselling by the new working relationship set up between the counselling centre and the residential unit.

Here we can see how, in order to understand the clients' problems and offer effective help, the counsellor had to think not only of the client as an individual, but also of the client's place in the referring organization. It soon became evident that this organization was in a state of conflict about the nature of its primary task: was it there primarily to promote the growth and development of the residents, or should it accept the limitations imposed by the severity of their mental illness and focus more on organizing their life in the institution in as effective and humane a way as possible? In the literature on the psychodynamics of organizations this conflict has been called one between two models of care: a horticultural vs. a warehousing model (Obholzer & Roberts, 1994, pp. 143–4). Each of these models presupposes a particular kind of culture, based either on promoting individual growth or helping individuals accept realistic limits, which in turn impacts on the kinds of boundaries maintained with outside organizations, and on the style of leadership. Once the counsellor was able to gain some understanding of these organizational dynamics, she could think of a way of intervening by working with the staff in order to help them clarify the competing models of care in operation. The staff were then in a position to work with the counsellor in establishing a better working relationship between the residential unit and the counselling centre.

Sometimes it is the dynamics not of another institution but of one's own that adversely affect the counsellor's ability to carry out his task.

A counsellor in a GP's surgery was employed by the practice to offer counselling to patients with emotional or psychological problems. All his referrals would come from the practice doctors. When the counsellor started he was careful to explain to all the doctors in the practice what counselling could offer to clients, and that it was essential to obtain the understanding and agreement of the client before making a referral. The counsellor also wrote a leaflet which explained what counselling was, and which he sent to each client referred with the initial appointment letter. Having laid the ground carefully for his work, he was then perplexed to find that many of the clients who came to see him said they had no idea why they had been referred and could not see how counselling could help them. For example, one client referred had complained persistently to his doctor of a constant pain in his stomach, but no physical cause could be found. He was angry about being referred to a 'shrink' as this clearly indicated to him that the doctor thought he was a 'malingerer'. Another client was referred after she had consulted her doctor about a fertility problem and had burst into tears in the surgery. However, she made it clear to the counsellor that her crying in the surgery was not because she was depressed, she had just been upset about not being able to

THE ORGANIZATIONAL FRAMEWORK

conceive on her own. She told the counsellor that she did not want counsel-
ling, she simply wanted the doctor to make a referral for fertility treatment.

With these and other similar clients the counsellor came to think that the
most accurate formulation of their problem was 'my doctor cannot cope with
me'. To be more precise, the situation with such a client might be something
like this, 'I have been referred because my doctor is at his/her wits end with
me, feels helpless or guilty at not being able to help me or cannot bear to see
me in pain anymore, or cannot cope with me when I express strong feelings
in the surgery, and needs someone to send me to who can take care of the
problem or, better still, make the problem go away'.

Eventually, as the inappropriate referrals continued, the counsellor real-
ized that he could not operate in splendid isolation from the demands of the
practice and the anxieties and defences of the referring doctors. He therefore
organized a meeting with the Practice Manager and, with her approval,
decided to meet with the referring doctors on a regular basis, where referrals
could be discussed. At these meetings it became clear how much pressure
the doctors were under. Some of the doctors realized how they were using
the counsellor to refer the patients they found most difficult rather than
those who might actually want and benefit from counselling. The counsellor
offered these doctors a chance to talk with him on a regular basis about these
more trying cases. As a result of these measures, the number of inappropri-
ate referrals to the counsellor was significantly reduced.

As in the previous example the counsellor found his role as a
counsellor affected and constricted by the institutional dynamics. He realized that he had come to fulfil an unconscious function for the referring doctors, namely a receptacle for the feelings
and anxieties about their work which they found hardest to bear.
In referring their most troublesome, intractable or most anxiety-
provoking patients, the doctors were unconsciously hoping to rid
themselves of their own feelings of irritation, helplessness or rage
which were stirred up by these patients. These disowned feelings
did not just disappear, however. Instead they continued to rever-
berate through the practice, affecting the counsellor, who felt irritated and de-skilled in the face of the inappropriate referrals, and
also the referred patients, who were angry about being passed from
one professional to another, and felt this must mean they were a
hopeless case.

This projective system continued as long as it remained out of
awareness. It was only when the counsellor finally spoke to the
practice manager, and then met the doctors as a group that he could
clearly see the enormous emotional pressure the doctors were under.

He came to appreciate that it was almost inevitable that they would see the counsellor as offering them some respite from their daily encounter with their patients' pain and unhappiness. Once this was acknowledged, at least by some of the doctors in the practice, they were able to think creatively about how the counsellor could support them directly by offering them some time to talk about their most difficult patients and how to manage their anxieties. These doctors were then able to think more realistically about which of their patients might actually benefit from counselling, and hence make more appropriate referrals.

The organization and the individual

The purpose of this chapter has been to demonstrate the need for an organizational perspective on counselling. Without such a point of view, the counsellors in both examples might have blamed themselves, or their clients, for the problems they encountered in their work. But paying attention to the organizational dynamics in play helped them to see that the difficulties lay not with them but in the wider system.

In some ways organizations, or their constituent parts, can be seen to function like individuals, beset by anxieties from which they need to defend themselves. In the two examples in this chapter, these anxieties were predominantly rooted in the painful or intolerable feelings stirred up in the staff by having to work with residents or patients who did not get better. In the residential unit these feelings were defended against, in part, by a never-ending dispute between the staff about the most appropriate model of care, in which feelings such as anger or disappointment with the residents could be displaced onto their colleagues. In the GP surgery the doctors invested the counsellor with the task of dealing with these intractable patients and so relieved them of having to face their painful feelings.

In some ways organizations also differ from individuals. Probably the most notable difference is that, as an organization consists of groups of individuals working together, it has a structure and a hierarchy. In the examples we can see how the counsellor needed to be given authority in order to intervene in the way the organization functioned. In the first example the counsellor worked alongside the manager of the unit, and in the second example, the counsellor first obtained the practice manager's blessing before he proceeded to arrange a meeting with the doctors.

In both examples an organizational perspective enabled the counsellor to move beyond thinking only in terms of the relationship with the client, from which perspective the counsellor was prone to blaming himself for the problems encountered in the work. Locating the source of the difficulty in a particular part of the wider organization allowed the counsellor to take active steps to intervene and change the dynamics, so that a better basis for the counselling could be established.

Looking to the organizational dimension may be felt to be alien to the very personal and intimate nature of therapeutic work, an unwelcome intrusion of an impersonal and bureaucratic way of thinking. It is true that bureaucratic thinking inevitably features in the work in any organization, for instance in the creation of client files so that information can be stored and tracked, or in the increasing demand for measurable outcome data so that services can be assessed and justified. But it can also seem like thinking of counselling in terms of the performance of a role or task is in itself a betrayal of its fundamental values. This is the spirit of a famous passage by Jean-Paul Sartre, in which he muses over the nature of human identity:

> Let us consider this waiter in the café. His movement is quick and forward, a little too precise, a little too rapid. He comes towards the patrons with a step a little too quick. He bends forward a little too eagerly; his voice, his eyes express an interest a little too solicitous for the order of the customer ... All his behaviour seems to us a game. He applies himself to chaining his movements as if they were mechanisms, the one regulating the others; his gestures and even his voice seem to be mechanisms; he gives himself the quickness and pitiless rapidity of things ... he is playing at being a waiter in a café. (Sartre, 1969, p. 59)

This description of how a person comes to establish an identity in the world by the way he performs his *metier* points to both a truth and a danger in being a counsellor. There is no doubt that psychodynamic work does have an impersonal or game-like quality in the way it establishes the boundaries of the work, marking it off from the more familial and friendship-based relationships in the client's life. Perhaps this is most evident when the counsellor explicitly eschews personal disclosure to the client. This rule-like quality is also there in the way the session is constructed, with its fixed boundaries of time and place, and in the whole relationship between counsellor and client, which is subordinated to the task of helping the client with her problems. The danger is that this necessary impersonality in the role can become too pronounced, so that the work itself can become mechanical, routine and boring. This is what happens when a counsellor becomes 'burnt out', he is then no longer able to take pleasure and be creative in his work.

But what the examples in this chapter show is that problems arise in the work not when people take up their role but when they don't. In the examples in this chapter the counsellors could have remained passive, which would have meant that they allowed themselves to be rendered ineffective as counsellors. Instead they drew on their counselling skills and organizational understanding in order to establish with their professional colleagues a viable setting for the work. In other words it is in taking up one's role in as thoughtful and vigorous way as possible that enables rather than prevents the worker from being effective and creative.

> To take a role is to be creative. In taking a role we 'enact' it. We make it come alive by publicly setting its limits and boundary. Simultaneously we lay claim to some hypothesis about the real world. We interpret reality, we give it coherence by placing bounds on our own potential and rejecting our fantasies of omnipotence. (Hirshhorn, 1985, p. 350)

Perhaps this is the hardest task in becoming a counsellor, time and time again having to come up against our limits and imperfections as we subordinate ourselves to the task of shaping our interventions in ways that the client might find useful.

Summary

An organizational perspective will help the counsellor understand some of the unconscious anxieties and defences in play in the institution or organization in which he works. Employing a wider conceptual framework than the one usually employed in counselling – involving concepts such as role, primary task, boundary, culture and leadership – can be essential for a counsellor whose work becomes affected by organizational dynamics, and can orient the counsellor to taking effective action in order to preserve or establish the integrity and viability of the counselling work.

Further reading

De Board, R (1978) *The Psychoanalysis of Organizations,* London: Tavistock.

Hinshelwood, R and Skogstad, W (2000) *Observing Institutions – Anxiety, Defence and Culture in Healthcare,* London: Routledge.

Huffington, C, Armstrong, D, Halton, W, Hoyle, L & Pooley, J (eds) (2004) *Working Below the Surface: the emotional life of contemporary organizations* London: Karnac Books.

Kegerreis, S (2001) 'Does "individual" have to mean "all on your own?" Integrating group-aware thinking in individual trainings', *Psychodynamic Practice* vol. 7, no. 3, pp. 261–78.

Menzies-Lyth, I (1984) *The Dynamics of the Social,* London: Free Association Books.

Noonan, E (1983) 'Counselling in organizations', Ch. 7 of *Counselling Young People,* London: Methuen.

Obholzer, A and Roberts, V (1994) *The Unconscious at Work,* London: Routledge.

REFERENCES

Aberbach, D (1989) *Surviving Trauma: Loss, Literature and Psychoanalysis,* New Haven: Yale University Press.

Balint, M (1968) *The Basic Fault,* London: Tavistock.

Bollas, C (1989) 'The trauma of incest', in *Forces of Destiny,* London: Free Association Books.

Bond, T (1993) 'Confidentiality', in *Standards and Ethics for Counselling in Action,* London: Sage.

Bowlby, J (1979) *The Making and Breaking of Affectional Bonds,* London: Routledge.

British Association of Counselling and Psychotherapy (2009) 'Ethical Framework', which incorporates 'Ethical Framework for Good Practice in Counselling and Psychotherapy', at www.bacp.co.uk.

Britton, R (1989) 'The missing link: parental sexuality in the Oedipus Complex', in *The Oedipus Complex Today,* ed. Britton, R, Feldman, M and O'Shaughnessy, E, London: Karnac Books.

Britton, R (1992) 'Keeping things in mind', in *Clinical Lectures on Klein and Bion,* ed. Anderson, R, London: Routledge.

Brown, D and Peddar, J (1979) *Introduction to Psychotherapy: an Outline of Psychodynamic Principles and Practice,* London: Tavistock.

Carpy, D (1989) 'Tolerating the countertransference: a mutative process', *International Journal of Psychoanalysis,* vol. 70, pp. 287–94.

Coren, A (2001) *Short-Term Psychotherapy: a Psychodynamic Approach,* London: Palgrave.

Ferenczi, S (1985) 'Confusion of tongues between adults and the child', in *The Assault on Truth* (Appendix C), ed. Masson, J, Harmondsworth: Penguin.

Forrester, J (1980) *Language and the Origins of Psychoanalysis,* London: Macmillan.

Freud, S (all references are to The Standard Edition of the Complete Psychological Works of Sigmund Freud, ed. Strachey, J, London: Hogarth).

Freud, S (1895) *Studies on Hysteria,* S.E.II.

Freud, S (1910) *Psychical Impotence in Men,* S.E.XI.

Freud, S (1911–13) *Papers on Technique,* S.E.XII.

Freud, S (1915) *Introductory Lectures on Psychoanalysis,* S.E.XV–XVI.

Freud, S (1917) *Mourning and Melancholia,* S.E.XIV.

Freud, S (1923) *The Ego and the Id*, S.E.XIX.

Freud, S (1925) *An Autobiographical Study*, S.E.XX.

Freud, S (1926) *The Question of Lay Analysis*, S.E.XX.

Gomez, L (1977) *An Introduction to Object Relations*, London: Free Association Books.

Green, A (1972) 'The analyst, symbolization and absence in the analytic setting', in *On Private Madness*, London: Hogarth.

Heimann, P (1950) 'On counter-transference', *International Journal of Psychoanalysis*, vol. 31, pp. 81–4.

Hirschhorn, L (1985) 'The psychodynamics of taking the role', ch. 13 of *The Group Relations Reader*, ed. Coleman, A and Geller, M, Washington: A.K. Rice Institute.

Holmes, J (1994) 'Attachment – a secure base for counselling?', *Psychodynamic Counselling*, vol. 1, no. 1, pp. 67–78.

Jacobs, M (1994) 'Psychodynamic counselling: an identity achieved?', *Psychodynamic Counselling*, vol. 1, no. 1, pp. 79–93.

Joseph, B (1989) 'Transference: the total situation', in *Psychic Equilibrium and Psychic Change*, London: Routledge.

Klauber, J (1986) *Difficulties in the analytic encounter*, Free Association Books: London.

Klein, M (1940) 'Mourning and its relation to manic-depressive states', in *The Selected Melanie Klein*, ed. Mitchell, J, 1986, Harmondsworth: Penguin.

Klein, M (1950) 'On the Criteria for the Termination of a Psycho-Analysis', in *Envy and Gratitude*, 1984, London: Hogarth.

Klein, M (1955) 'On Identification', in *Envy and Gratitude*, 1984, London: Hogarth.

Malan, D (1979) *Individual Psychotherapy and the Science of Psychodynamics*, London: Butterworths.

Nicholas, J (1992) 'The inside story: on seeing clients in their own homes', in *The Making of a Counsellor*, ed. Noonan, E and Spurling, L, London: Routledge.

Obholzer A and Roberts V (1994) *The Unconscious at Work*, London: Routledge.

Ogden, T (1992) *The Primitive Edge of Experience*, London: Maresfield Library.

O'Shaughnessy, E (1989) 'The Invisible Oedipus Complex', in *The Oedipus Complex Today*, ed. Britton, R, Feldman, M and O'Shaughnessy, E, London: Karnac Books.

O'Shaughnessy, E (1992) 'Psychosis: not thinking in a bizarre world', in *Clinical Lectures on Klein and Bion*, ed. Anderson, R, London: Routledge.

Parkes, C (1975) *Bereavement: Studies of Grief in Adult Life*, Harmondsworth: Penguin.

Pearson, K (1995) 'Problems with transference interpretation in short-term dynamic psychotherapy', *British Journal of Psychotherapy*, vol. 12, no. 1, pp. 37–48.

Pincus, L and Dare, C (1978) *Secrets in the Family*, London: Faber & Faber.

Quinodoz, D (1992) 'The psychoanalytic setting as the instrument of the container function', *International Journal of Psychoanalysis*, vol. 73, pp. 627–35.

Racker, H (1985) *Transference and Counter-transference*, London: Maresfield Library.

Rosenfeld, H (1987) *Impasse and Interpretation*, London: Routledge.

Rycroft, C (1988) *Anxiety and Neurosis*, London: Maresfield Library.

Sartre, J-P (1969) *Being and Nothingness*, Methuen: London.

Searles, H (1979) *Countertransference and Related Subjects*, International University Press: New York.

Searles, H (1994) *My Work with Borderline Patients*, Northvale, NJ: Jason Aronson.

Sennett, R (2008) *The Craftsman*, Allen Lane: London.

Segal, H (1964) *An Introduction to the Work of Melanie Klein*, London: Hogarth.

Segal, H (1988) 'Notes on symbol formation', in *Melanie Klein Today, vol. 1, Mainly Theory*, ed. Spillius, E, London: Routledge.

Spurling, L (2003) 'On the therapeutic value of not offering psychotherapy: an account of an extended assessment', *Psychoanalytic Psychotherapy*, vol. 17, no. 1, pp. 1–17.

Symington, J and Symington, N (1996) *The Clinical Thinking of Wilfred Bion*, London: Routledge.

Tame, J (1996) 'The seductiveness of theory: counselling in dyads and triads in a case history', *Psychodynamic Counselling*, vol. 2, no. 1, pp. 39–54.

Tolstoy, L (1960) *The Death of Ivan Illych and Other Stories*, Harmondsworth: Penguin.

Turner, V (1967) *The Forest of Symbols*, Ithaca: Cornell University Press.

Waddell, M (1998) *Inside Lives: Psychoanalysis and the Growth of the Personality*, London: Duckworth.

Winnicott, D (1936) 'Appetite and emotional disorder', in *Through Paediatrics to Psychoanalysis*, 1978, London: Hogarth.

Winnicott, D (1941) 'The observation of infants in a set situation, in *Through Paediatrics to Psychoanalysis*, 1978, London: Hogarth

Winnicott, D (1951) 'Transitional objects and transitional phenomena', in *Through Paediatrics to Psychoanalysis*, 1978, London: Hogarth.

Winnicott, D (1954) 'Metapsychological and clinical aspects of regression within the psychoanalytical set-up', in *Through Paediatrics to Psychoanalysis*, 1978, London: Hogarth.

Winnicott, D (1964) 'What do we mean by a normal child?', in *The Child, the Family and the Outside World*, 1964, Harmondsworth: Penguin.

Winnicott, D (1971) *Therapeutic Consultations in Child Psychiatry*, London: Hogarth.

Winnicott, D (1986) 'The concept of a healthy individual', in *Home is Where We Start From*, Harmondsworth: Penguin.

INDEX

absence (as feature of more disturbed
    clients), 89, 148
acting out, 64, 96, 118, 119, 155, 159
    see also enactment
aggression, 76, 100, 136
agoraphobia, 56, 77, 82
    and claustrophobia, 77
    see also phobic defence
ambivalence, 62, 79, 80, 84, 90, 95
annihilation, 148, 149
anorexia, 12
    see also appetite, disorders of
anxiety, 37, 40, 43, 48, 49, 50, 52, 53, 55,
      56, 70, 73, 77, 79, 81, 89, 90, 107, 118,
      127, 128, 135, 138, 139, 141, 143, 159,
      167, 171, 174
    depressive, 74–84
    organizational, 168
    persecutory (paranoid-schizoid),
      77–83
appetite, disorders of, 69–74
    see also anorexia; bulimia
arrogance, 111, 114
assessment, 124, 125–8, 129, 130, 139,
      142, 143, 144, 162, 174
attachment, 48, 50, 51, 52, 55, 58, 76,
      79, 173
attachment theory, 50
authority, 12, 13, 17, 24, 43, 47, 105, 159,
      162, 163, 168

beginning of session, 43
beginning phase, 2, 30, 123–32,
      134, 144
Bereavement: Studies of Grief in Adult Life,
      49, 173
Bion, W, 20, 22, 149, 172, 173, 174
borderline personality or state, 2, 148,
      153–8, 159, 160, 174
breakdown
    fear of, 155
    risk of, 158

breaks in counselling schedule, *see*
    under temporal aspects of
    setting
Breuer, J, 13
brief counselling, 31, 140–3
British Association of Counselling
    and Psychotherapy, 1, 3, 45
Britton, R, 20, 21, 83, 84, 145, 172, 173
bulimia, 71–4, 77, 81, 119
    see also appetite, disorders of

catharsis, 11, 95
Charcot, J, 12–13
child abuse, 32
compliance, 97, 114, 146, 154
compulsion, 88, 104, 107
concern, 8, 157
confidentiality, 3, 31, 32–3, 39, 44, 172
conflict, 12, 13, 15, 16, 17, 18, 34, 35, 40,
      42, 45, 51, 55, 58, 66, 73, 87, 89, 90,
      96, 121, 122, 126, 130, 133, 139,
      164, 166
confusion, 64, 81, 106, 107, 108, 124, 172
containment, 2, 20–3, 24, 25, 26, 28,
      30, 36, 41, 44, 46, 84, 95, 98,
      113, 118, 120, 122, 128, 148, 152,
      158, 159
contamination, 79
contempt, 59, 99, 114
contract, 27, 28, 31–3, 37–8, 99, 100, 103,
      106, 128, 138, 140
control, 41, 55, 57, 70, 71, 74, 76, 77,
      78, 80, 83, 96, 104, 105, 106, 111,
      119, 133
counselling relationship, 2, 3, 28, 31, 32,
      47, 83, 92, 93, 95, 96, 98, 106, 108,
      118, 119, 120, 121, 122, 133, 142, 155,
      158, 161, 162, 169
    see also transference
counsellor's attitude and behaviour
    as part of setting, 27, 28, 31,
      33–6

counter-transference, 111–16, 122, 131, 152, 155, 156, 158, 159, 173, 174
    see also transference
counter-transference position, 114
counter-transference reactions, 113, 114, 115, 152, 155, 156, 158, 159
cultural and ethnic differences, 108, 122

Death of Ivan Ilyich, 8
defence, 15, 51, 52, 54, 55, 56, 57, 75, 76, 77, 78, 79, 80, 82, 89, 99, 111, 134, 138, 144, 147, 150, 153, 156, 159, 167, 170, 171, 174
    see also under individual defences:
        denial; displacement; evacuation; hysterical defence; idealization; manic defence; obsessional defence; omnipotence; phobic defence; projection; projective identification; repression; splitting; turning round (thoughts/feelings) against oneself
delusion, 117, 148
denial, 37, 80, 83, 134, 156
dependence, 15, 16, 17, 18, 51, 72, 76, 157
depression, 37, 38, 50, 52, 57–9, 81, 94, 103, 126, 129, 130, 131, 134, 155
depressive position or mode of experience, 75–83, 91, 127, 132, 136, 137
    and the Oedipus Complex, 83–5
    see also paranoid-schizoid position
deprivation, 140, 147
developmental point of view, 46–7, 49, 50–2, 89
diagnosis, 150, 158, 159
displacement, 56, 58, 93
dissociation, 79, 147, 148, 154, 156
    see also splitting
dreaming, 147
duration of counselling, see under temporal aspects of setting

ego, 57–9, 147, 149, 153
ego-strength, 92
emotional sensibility of counsellor, 112, 114
empathy, 18, 23

emptiness, feeling of, 72, 73, 81, 148
enactment, 17, 39, 41, 74, 77, 113, 119, 121, 123
    see also acting out
end phase, 134–40, 142, 144,
engagement with client, 18, 144, 146
envy, 108, 132, 139, 173
erotic transference, 98, 102–7, 116, 122
eroticized transference, 106–7
"Ethical Framework for Good Practice in Counselling and Psychotherapy", 3, 172
ethics, 3, 45, 172
evacuation, 70, 77

fantasy, 30, 59, 70
    see also phantasy
Ferenczi, S, 64, 172
financial arrangements in counselling, 28, 33
first session, 29, 101, 128–30, 136, 144
fragmentation, 80, 147, 148, 149, 154
frequency of sessions, see under temporal aspects of setting
Freud, S, 3, 4, 12, 13, 19, 27, 41, 51, 55, 56, 57, 58, 59, 60, 62, 63, 84, 87, 95, 96, 98, 111, 153, 172, 173
frustration, toleration of, 51, 62, 75, 97, 121, 149, 153

gender identity, 61, 84–7
    see also under Oedipus Complex
greed, 73, 74, 76, 101, 140
grief, 37, 38, 48–50, 52, 75, 76, 90, 173
    normal/pathological, 50–1
    stages of, 50
guilt, 6, 49, 50, 75, 76, 79, 136, 137, 157, 167

hallucination, 70, 148
health and illness, 51
Heimann, P. 112, 113, 173
holding, 22, 23, 45, 162
homosexuality
    (and heterosexuality), 108–9
hypnosis, 95
hysteria, 12
hysterical defence, 57

id, 57
idealization, 44, 97, 100, 101, 102, 135, 136, 138
idealizing transference, 100–2, 103
identification, 2, 57–9, 60, 61, 62, 64, 77, 80, 87, 88, 90, 102, 128, 173
If I Were You, 88
impasse, 101, 118, 143, 174
impotence, 62, 172
incest, 63–4, 107, 117, 172
institutional setting, 32, 158, 159
    see also organizational framework
internal object, 67, 68–74, 75, 79, 90, 121, 157
internal (*or* inner) world, 68–74, 75, 79, 83, 84, 90, 92, 101, 121, 161
internalization, 63, 68
interpretation, 18, 19, 23, 44, 53, 66, 74, 92, 99, 101, 110, 112, 116, 117, 119, 120, 127, 136, 139, 152, 156, 157
    see also transference, interpretation
Introductory Lectures on Psychoanalysis, 19, 52, 172

jealousy, 61, 64, 66, 84, 87

Klein, M, 25, 46, 68, 69, 74–6, 78, 87, 88, 90, 91, 107, 135, 172, 173, 174

leadership, 163
length of sessions, *see under* temporal aspects of setting
life cycle, 51–2
listening, 13, 24, 33, 76, 110, 113, 130
loss, 13, 31, 41, 48–50, 51, 57, 58, 74–6, 79, 81, 90, 123, 125, 136, 137, 140, 153, 157, 172

manic defences, 76
manic reparation, 76
manic states, 134, 173
melancholia, *see* depression
mental processes, 52, 57
middle phase, 123, 132–4, 143, 144
modes of generating experience, 90
mourning, *see* grief
mutuality, 17, 154

narcissism, 148, 153, 158, 159
negative transference, 96, 97, 98–102, 103, 105, 106, 114, 118, 121, 157
neurosis, 60, 153, 174
neutrality, attitude of, 28, 35

object, 53, 56, 57, 58, 59, 61, 77, 79, 80, 81, 84, 85, 90, 92, 102, 108, 120, 121, 122, 133, 135, 146, 148, 149, 153, 157, 158, 159, 174
    change of (in Oedipus Complex), 84–7
    choice, 62
    good/bad, 73–5, 80
    part/whole, 79
    see also internal object; object relationship; transitional object
object relationship, 73, 90, 92, 98, 101, 107, 110, 111, 113, 121,
observing the client, 110
obsessional defence, 56
Oedipal
    barrier, 107, *see also* incest
    father, 85
    feelings, 61, 62, 64, 86
    figures, 68
    framework, 117
    mother, 67, 85
    scenario, 96
    schema, 63, 83, 95, 161
    triangle, 84
    see also pre-oedipal
Oedipus Complex, 2, 59–67, 68, 89, 90, 172, 173
    and the depressive position, 82–4
    early stages of and gender identity, 84–7
Oedipus Rex, 87
omnipotence, 85, 153, 170
On Identification, 87, 173
organizational framework, 4, 32, 161–70
    see also anxiety, organizational; institutional setting
O'Shaughnessy, E, 149, 172, 173
over-determination, 41

paranoid-schizoid position or mode of experience, 77–82, 83, 84, 87, 90–1, 145, 148, 153, 157, 159
    see also anxiety, persecutory; depressive position

Parkes, C, 49, 173
phantasy, 71, 78, 80
    see also fantasy
phases of counselling, 2, 123–44
phobic defence, 48, 56, 57
pining, 49, 76
positive transference, 97, 100, 106, 121, 154, 157, 158, 159
pre-occupation, 20
pre-Oedipal, 83, 84, 85, 86
    see also Oedipal
primary task, 162–3
professional network, 32, 156, 158
projection, 56, 78, 95, 107, 108, 115, 121, 133, 149, 157, 159
projective identification, 12, 77, 80, 88, 102
projective system (in an organization), 167
psychoanalysis, 1, 3, 4, 11, 19, 22, 24, 27, 51, 52, 91, 111, 137, 171, 172, 173, 174
psychoanalytic psychotherapy, 3, 4, 174
psychodynamic, 1, 2, 23, 24
Psychodynamic Practice, 3, 91, 122, 160, 171
psychosis, 2, 117, 118, 148–53, 154, 159, 160, 173

reality-testing, 121
reassurance, 8, 34, 132, 138
referral of clients, 2, 124–5, 144, 158, 162, 163, 165, 166, 167
reparation, 76, 79
    see also manic reparation
repetition, 11, 18, 31, 96, 98, 104, 122, 123, 141
    see also transference, and repetition
representation, 54
repression, 52, 55–6, 60, 80, 89
resistance, 24, 89, 96
retaliation, 76, 77, 93
revelation (in paranoid-schizoid mode of experience), 80
reverie, 22
ritual healing, 9–12, 18
role of counsellor, 12, 36, 63, 73, 167
role in organizations, 162, 169, 170, 173
Rosenfeld, H, 117, 145, 174

sado-masochism, 116
schizophrenia, 78, 117, 145, 150
Searles, H, 80, 81, 134, 174
Segal, H, 78, 91, 174
self-destructive behaviour, 72, 155, 156, 157, 159
setting, 2, 4, 9, 10, 11, 21, 26–45, 46, 47, 92, 98, 99, 102, 116, 117, 118, 123, 144, 153, 158, 159, 161, 170, 173, 174
    accommodation to, 37–43
    as set situation, 36–7, 174
    see also counsellor's attitude and behaviour as part of setting; spatial aspects of setting; temporal aspects of setting
sexual abuse, 60, 63–4, 106, 107, 172
sexuality, 54–7, 104, 105, 107, 172
    see also erotic transference
sexual/pre-sexual body, 55, 83
Sophocles, 61, 87
spatial aspects of setting, 27–9, 45
splitting, 77, 79–80, 148, 157
    see also dissociation
Squiggle Game, 14–20, 146
stealing, 146, 147
Studies on Hysteria, 13, 172
subjectivity, 81
sublimation, 62, 78
suicide, *see* self-destructive behaviour
superego, 57, 63
supervision, 115, 117, 122, 131
symbol formation, 174
symbolic, 11, 12, 13, 15, 17, 28, 53, 54, 85, 118
    and real, 28, 36, 63–4
    equation, 78, 81, 107, 117
symbolization, 54, 85, 90, 118, 173
symptoms, 12, 13, 49, 52, 53, 57, 89, 130, 131, 158

temporal aspects of setting, 27, 29–31, 45
    breaks in schedule, 43–4, 82, 93, 99, 103
    duration of counselling, 27, 30, 31
    frequency of sessions, 4, 27, 30, 113, 128
    length of session, 27, 29, 38–41, 162
    schedule of sessions, 27, 41–3, 93

theory, 2, 13, 18, 25, 48, 52
  and belief, 87–9
  psychoanalytic, 46, 50, 52
  purpose of, 46–7
therapeutic
  conversation, 7
  consultation, 14–20, 29, 145–8, 174
  dialogue, 13, 14–20, 24, 34
  process, 11, 26
Therapeutic Consultations in Child Psychiatry, 14, 174
therapy, personal
  (as part of training), 115
time-limited counselling, 4, 31, 134, 140–4
Tolstoy, I, 8, 17, 174
total situation, *see under* transference
training as a psychodynamic counsellor, 4, 115, 117, 122, 149, 160, 171
transference, 17, 74, 92–122, 174
  of counsellor onto client, 111, 115
  as creation of counsellor and client, 115–16, 161
  discovery of, 95–7
  interpretation, 117–22
  organizational, 162
  personal element in, 95
  prevailing pattern of, 113, 122
  recognition of, 110–11, 113, 114
  and repetition, 96
  social dimension of, 107–9, 123
  symbolic nature of, 159
  thinking in, 116

as total situation, 107, 173
  working in, 2, 110–22
  see also counselling relationship;
    counter-transference;
    erotic transference;
    eroticized transference;
    idealizing transference; negative transference;
    positive transference
transitional object, 85
trauma, 13, 57, 59, 60, 89, 95, 99, 100, 174
triangular space or structure, 64, 84, 161
triumph, 13, 67, 76
Turner, V, 9, 10, 11, 12, 13, 174
turning round (of feelings/thoughts) against oneself, 56

unconscious, 25, 55, 64, 69, 74, 85, 89, 112, 128
  communication, 112, 131
  phantasy, *see* phantasy

valency, 115

Winnicott, D, 14–20, 23, 27, 29, 36, 46, 51, 52, 69, 70, 71, 85, 141, 142, 145–8, 174
withdrawal, 49, 58, 87, 94, 148
working alliance, 97, 99, 107, 119, 120, 121, 123, 128, 130, 132, 133, 142, 144, 148, 154, 158
working in the transference, *see under* transference
working-through, 19, 24, 135, 137, 141